PUFF

MY

A.P.J. Abdul Kalam was one of India's most distinguished scientists, responsible for the development of the country's first satellite launch vehicle and the operationalization of strategic missiles. He also pioneered India Vision 2020, a road map for transforming India. The President of India between 2002 and 2007, Dr Kalam was awarded honorary doctorates from thirty-eight universities and the country's three highest civilian honours—the Padma Bhushan (1981), Padma Vibhushan (1990) and Bharat Ratna (1997). A prolific and bestselling author, he conducted lectures on societal development in many international institutes and was involved in research on different societal missions. Dr Kalam passed away in July 2015.

Also in Puffin by A.P.J. Abdul Kalam

Mission India: A Vision for Indian Youth
Reignited: Scientific Pathways to a Brighter Future

MY INDIA
Ideas for the future

A.P.J. Abdul Kalam

Foreword by Srijan Pal Singh
Research by Shrutkeerti Khurana

PUFFIN BOOKS

PUFFIN BOOKS
Published by the Penguin Group
Penguin Books India Pvt. Ltd, 7th Floor, Infinity Tower C, DLF Cyber City, Gurgaon 122 002, Haryana, India
Penguin Group (USA) Inc., 375 Hudson Street, New York, New York 10014, USA
Penguin Group (Canada), 90 Eglinton Avenue East, Suite 700, Toronto, Ontario, M4P 2Y3, Canada
Penguin Books Ltd, 80 Strand, London WC2R 0RL, England
Penguin Ireland, 25 St Stephen's Green, Dublin 2, Ireland (a division of Penguin Books Ltd)
Penguin Group (Australia), 707 Collins Street, Melbourne, Victoria 3008, Australia
Penguin Group (NZ), 67 Apollo Drive, Rosedale, Auckland 0632, New Zealand
Penguin Books (South Africa) (Pty) Ltd, Block D, Rosebank Office Park, 181 Jan Smuts Avenue, Parktown North, Johannesburg 2193, South Africa

Penguin Books Ltd, Registered Offices: 80 Strand, London WC2R 0RL, England

First published in Puffin by Penguin Books India 2015

Copyright © A.P.J. Adbul Kalam 2014
Foreword copyright © Srijan Pal Singh 2015

All rights reserved

10 9 8 7 6 5 4 3 2 1

The views and opinions expressed in this book are the author's own and the facts are as reported by him/her which have been verified to the extent possible, and the publishers are not in any way liable for the same.

ISBN 9780143333531

Typeset in Minion Pro by Manipal Digital Systems, Manipal
Printed at Thomson Press India Ltd, New Delhi

This book is sold subject to the condition that it shall not, by way of trade or otherwise, be lent, resold, hired out, or otherwise circulated without the publisher's prior written consent in any form of binding or cover other than that in which it is published and without a similar condition including this condition being imposed on the subsequent purchaser and without limiting the rights under copyright reserved above, no part of this publication may be reproduced, stored in or introduced into a retrieval system, or transmitted in any form or by any means (electronic, mechanical, photocopying, recording or otherwise), without the prior written permission of both the copyright owner and the above-mentioned publisher of this book.

A PENGUIN RANDOM HOUSE COMPANY

Contents

Foreword   vii

Love Your Country   1

Lessons for Life   45

Dream Your Dreams   79

To Give Is to Gain   117

Failure Is a Teacher   149

Life Is Beautiful   173

Foreword

It is a difficult and rare honour for me to write a foreword for a book authored by my guru, the teacher of teachers—Dr A.P.J. Abdul Kalam (1931-2015). His ideas are far too vast and his vision too deep to be summarized or qualified in a small stretch of pages by this humble student of his. However, writing these words brings a wave of memories tinged with colours of intense emotion to my heart and mind. I am reminded of all those thoughts that my guru sparked and how each thought made me learn, evolve and transform. It makes me so proud that I shared many years, working so closely, with one of the greatest human beings who ever lived.

My journey with Dr Kalam began in September 2008 when I first saw him as a teacher. During my second year at the Indian Institute of Management, Ahmedabad, he was my professor for a course on nation building. On my final day with him, 27 July 2015, he remained a teacher, this time at the other end of the country, as a professor at the Indian Institute of Management, Shillong, taking a course on creating a liveable planet.

Foreword

Between 2008 and 2015, I have seen the infinity of his wisdom and the sensitivity and humility with which he lived his life. I have attended countless lectures of his, travelled extensively with him, listened to the numerous thoughts he's shared. I have shared walks and lunch-and-dinner conversations, and heard him call me a student, a friend, a co-author and often just 'funny guy'. In each of these associations, he ignited new thoughts, encouraged new actions and taught me that all failures, howsoever immense, are only temporary.

Dr A.P.J. Abdul Kalam's greatest legacy is the generations of Indians he has inspired to dream, excel and rise. The story of a newspaper boy rising to become a space scientist, rocket engineer, missile expert and eventually the eleventh President of India has given his countrymen the hope that hard work and talent do pay in the long run. It has also shown millions of Indians that the choices and effort one makes in life can conquer any odds or disadvantages of birth. I remember a professor in Australia once introducing Dr Kalam to his class saying, 'Even in his eighties, for the youth of India, he commands the respect of a sage and the charisma of a rock star.'

Dr Kalam had a special affinity with the youth. I remember him saying many a time, 'Up to the age of seventeen, the mind of a youth can be shaped. Beyond that it becomes difficult.' Hence, he dedicated a large part of his time, during his presidency and after that as well, to shaping the mind of the Indian youth. He wanted them to have three traits—righteousness, creativity and courage. He even gave it the form of an equation, which he called the 'Knowledge Equation', where knowledge is defined as the sum of these three traits. And of course, he famously said, 'Knowledge makes you great'. With three simple words, he outlined the pathway to greatness. Such was the simplicity of Dr Kalam.

I was a part of the creation of many of Dr Kalam's speeches covered in this book. Each piece was intensely researched, composed, rejected and then re-composed before it came to its final form. Dr Kalam would sit across the table with the computer as the text of the speech was projected on a wall of the small office. We would debate every single idea and thought that would go into the speech. Version after version would come up and in some cases, we'd have more than twenty versions of a speech!

Dr Kalam was very particular about his audience and he would always ask, 'Is this lecture going to inspire all the listeners? Will it be interesting for the people present?' These carefully selected words would then be delivered with craftsmanship by Dr Kalam, igniting the audience's dreams every single time. He had a way of engaging his listeners and making them all feel important and capable of contributing to a cause rather than merely being the audience at a speech.

Each chapter in this book brings alive a precious memory for me. The extract titled 'Birth of a World Leader' captures how Dr Kalam saw the life of Gandhiji in South Africa, and was amongst the first lectures I heard him give back in 2008, when I was a student. He told me about his experience in

Foreword

Kibutu in Arunachal Pradesh (in the extract 'Jai Hind') during one of our dinner discussions in Raj Bhawan, Itanagar, while looking on at the Himalayas. This became a prominent story in one of the books we co-authored—*Target 3 Billion*.

The extract 'Kidney Chain' reminds me of the exact manner of how Dr Kalam reacted and how deeply he was touched when he learned that the well-known industrialist Shri Kochouseph Chittilappilly donated his kidney to an unknown ailing driver. The conversation between Dr Kalam and Shri Chittilappilly indeed had a significant impact, not only on both Dr Kalam and Chittilappilly but also on everybody else who learned about this incident through Dr Kalam's lectures.

Most poignantly, the hymn 'Righteousness of the Heart' in the extract 'Happiness of the Whole' were the exact words Dr Kalam was about to say standing at the lectern at IIM Shillong when he left us.

People often ask me now, 'Was Dr Kalam ever worried about the state of the nation? Was he worried about how corruption hampers growth or how pollution degrades human life?' The answer is an unequivocal 'Yes, of course.' But at the same time, he was a perennial optimist and had an unflinching faith in the ability and intent of the Indian youth to overcome every single problem the nation faces. He trusted the youth to think of fresh ideas and generate innovations and create a brand of integrity in all their actions.

This book, a collection of his thoughts, largely focused on the youth and articulated at different moments of his life, is indeed an important milestone in motivating and energizing the youth to the position to which they truly belong—as the foremost nation builders.

Today, Dr Kalam is not with us in a mortal form. But great personalities never perish; they just transform from human form to powerful ideas. Dr Kalam as an idea is and will always be alive with us and *My India: Ideas for the Future* is a commendable effort towards it. I commend Puffin India and the team for their diligence in bringing this book out despite the difficult times following Dr Kalam's sudden passing.

I am confident that this book will help young readers understand Dr Kalam much better and give them the confidence, motivation and courage to continue on the path he showed us all. I am also confident that they will work towards fulfilling many of Dr Kalam's yet-to-be completed dreams, which include creating an economically developed India by 2020, ensuring that rural areas develop, bringing transparency and integrity in all walks of life and establishing India as a knowledge superpower.

In August 2015, a week after Dr Kalam's sudden demise, I was in Chennai, where I was talking to a small group of children from a government school. I asked them, 'When you grow up, what would you like to be?' They all spontaneously raised their hands and cheered, 'Kalam!' Such was his effect on the youth of this nation.

Indeed, for the rest of my life, like millions of youth of India, 'Kalam sir' will never cease to exist. Through his lectures and dreams, he continues to inspire us, ignite our imaginations and

Foreword

push us far beyond the boundaries our minds had perceived for our potential.

As I conclude, I would like to share a few words I came across while reading this book. A poem by the great Mizo poet Rukunga, titled 'The World of Parting', was sung to Dr Kalam by a group of children in Mizoram in 2005:

> *'Now we part with a heavy and painful heart,*
> *The world we live in, has been destined for parting,*
> *By the heavenly father above . . .'*

New Delhi   Srijan Pal Singh
November 2015

Love Your Country

'Dr Kalam was a fine and senior guide (marg darshak). I got the opportunity to work very closely with him. In my personal life, I have lost the best guide. The country has lost a son who worked to make our country a strong nation. He gave every moment to make India's youth strong and self-reliant.'

Narendra Modi, Prime Minister of India

The Birth of a World Leader

Address at the Gandhi Jayanti celebration, Orlando, USA

30 September 2012

My personal experiences around Gandhiji go back to 2004 when I was visiting South Africa to address the South African Parliament and the Pan-African Parliament with fifty-three members. One of the programmes organized during my visit included travelling from Durban to Pietermaritzburg. This visit was simulated to be like 1893 when Mahatma Gandhi travelled from Durban to Pietermaritzburg in a train hauled by a steam engine.

It was from Durban station that Gandhiji embarked on the fateful journey that later is regarded as having changed the course of his life. He boarded the train on 7 June 1893 to travel to Pretoria, where he was due to meet clients. A first-class seat had been booked for him. The train reached Pietermaritzburg station at about 9 p.m. A white passenger entering the compartment could not stomach a coloured person travelling with him. So he went out and returned with two officials who ordered Gandhiji to move to the van compartment. Later, a white constable was called who took Gandhiji by the hand and pushed him out of the train. His luggage was also removed and the train continued its journey without him. Gandhiji spent the night in the waiting room. It was winter and it was bitterly cold. And although his overcoat was in the luggage, Gandhiji did not ask for it, fearing further insults.

When I alighted at the Pietermaritzburg railway station, I saw a plaque that reads thus:

In the vicinity of this plaque, M.K. Gandhi was evicted from a first-class compartment on the night of 7 June 1893. This incident changed the course of his life. He took up the fight against racial oppression. His active non-violence started from that date.

Now, while looking at the plaque, I visualized the feelings and thoughts that would have gone through Gandhiji's mind on that fateful day. He was in the Pietermaritzburg railway station from 9 p.m. to 6 a.m. During this time, multiple thoughts were racing through his mind. Between 9 p.m. and 12 p.m., one of the thoughts taking shape was 'I must punish the oppressors'. Then, between 12 a.m. and 3 a.m., a second wave of thoughts came to him, which directed him 'I should leave South Africa and the practice of law and go back home to India and lead a happy life'. Between 3 a.m. and 6 a.m., a third wave of thoughts emerged, thoughts that led to a great decision: 'What can I give to Africa to help remove apartheid using the lessons of Pietermaritzburg?' That is how, on 7 June 1893, the seeds of the Satyagraha movement were planted, which finally led India to realize its freedom.

Jai Hind

Valedictory address to the Higher Defence Management Course, College of Defence Management, Hyderabad

22 March 2012

In the last year of my presidency in 2007, the Chief of the Army, General Joginder Jaswant Singh, strongly urged me to visit the Chinese border in the north-eastern state of Arunachal Pradesh. The General, popularly known as 'General JJ', is a veteran with a strong, overwhelming personality and an evergreen smile. So when JJ insisted that I address our soldiers at the border, I couldn't refuse. We arrived at a place called Kibutu at the frontier where the Chinese and Indian territories meet. We were in a valley, on the Indian side, with mountains reaching the skies around us.

On the other side, at a slightly higher altitude than ours, I could see the Chinese posts, where a few curious Chinese soldiers had gathered around. They were probably attracted by the commotion on the Indian side created by our visit. I looked at our young soldiers and the locals who had assembled there and then looked at the Himalayan mountains towering above. I was touched by the sheer amount of hardship the soldiers were going through in these difficult weather conditions. No matter what support we create for our soldiers, the hard reality of a Himalayan battlefield is that the weather is more often a bigger adversary than the enemy.

Then I looked at the local people assembled there, who were largely tribal. Their cheerful faces and smiles were not enough to conceal the most obvious signs of poverty and hardships: overworked hands, worn-out clothes and frail bodies. These frontier dwellers of India live in such adversity, often without any special assistance, and undertake a number of support and logistical roles for the army. As I walked past them, I heard the usual greeting in these tribal areas: an enthusiastic 'Jai Hind'.

I then addressed an integrated army command, with all the soldiers and officers, and I encountered their enthusiasm for the work in difficult situations; they are ever-ready to face any challenge, whether from across the border or from the weather. When I saw a number of young officers after my address, I said to them, 'Friends! Brave officers and men of India! I realize that you are working day and night for the peace and safety of the nation and its people. I am proud of all of you. Can each of you young men share with me one of your most cherished dreams?' There was a moment of silence and then several hands went up. A young soldier rose and saluted me smartly, before saying in a loud voice, 'Sir, whenever I see the Chinese in the Himalayas, I am reminded of my visit to Tawang. My utmost ambition is to fight and defeat any aggression by the Chinese.'

Another young officer added, 'Sir, my ambition in life is to recover the 50,000 square kilometres of land belonging to India from Chinese possession. I will fight till my last breath to get back this land.' Hearing him, the locals assembled burst into applause and starting chanting 'Jai Hind! Jai Hind!' at the top of their voices.

I was amazed by the spirit of the officers, soldiers and the locals and their resolve towards their nation. I am sure each one of you will have some such ambition in your heart that you would like to fulfil during your service to the nation.

Reaching the Unreached

Address at the launch of the M.B. Arogyagramam Primary Healthcare and M.B. Global Health Village Project, Mahabubnagar

29 March 2013

I would like to share an inspiring story of how, for the last twenty-five years, a single doctor has put all his dreams and efforts into bringing the tribal citizens of Karnataka into the mainstream. His efforts have been channelled through the Vivekananda Girijana Kalyana Kendra at B R Hills in south Karnataka. When I visited B R Hills in 1998 and then subsequently in 2006, I could see many substantial new developments in that area. I could see that a new hospital for tribals had been built; and roads and the education environment and, above all, the earning capacity of the tribal citizens had been increased with the technology resource centre as a base. Dr H. Sudarshan is the inspiring architect of this societal transformation.

When Dr Sudarshan was only twelve years old, his father died in a village without any medical help. Shortly after, Dr Sudarshan read the biography of Dr Albert Schweitzer, who worked in Africa, which motivated Dr Sudarshan to take up the medical profession and work in the tribal areas of India. Dr Sudarshan derives his philosophy of work from Swami Vivekananda's teachings, which state: 'They alone live who live for others; the rest are more dead than alive.'

Dr Sudarshan starts his day at 4.30 a.m. with yoga, meditation and prayer with tribal schoolchildren. After his breakfast at 7.30 a.m., he attends to administrative work for an hour. From 9 a.m. to 1 p.m., he goes around the ward and sees the patients individually. He has lunch with the tribal students between 1 p.m. and 2 p.m. Until 7 p.m., he is busy in his clinic where he conducts minor surgeries. Later, he does more administrative work for an hour and a half and then has dinner with the tribal students. He devotes one hour to study, from 9 p.m. to 10 p.m., so that he is up to date on information about medical systems and other subjects. He spends a large part of his time in clinical diagnosis, laboratory diagnosis and treatment, in addition to supervising, monitoring, teaching and carrying out research along with his team members.

Dr Sudarshan pays particular attention to the special problems of the tribals such as snakebite cases, mauling by bears, pneumonia, tuberculosis and acute respiratory infections. The Soliga tribal people of southern Karnataka suffer from sickle-cell anaemia and Dr Sudarshan has developed a low-cost electrophoresis machine to diagnose the disease. He has also built the healthcare system on the strengths of traditional knowledge available in the tribal areas. The secret of his service is that he is empowering the people to manage their own health by giving them knowledge. He has trained tribal girls as auxiliary nurses and midwives (ANMs) and posted them in tribal sub-centres. These nurses undergo an eighteen-month course and are fully trained. Thus, this rural area is self-sufficient in terms of nursing resources.

Dr Sudarshan has also developed a low-cost management system for epilepsy in the primary healthcare centre (PHC). He has introduced dental healthcare and cancer control in the PHC. He provides quality healthcare to the people by introducing low-premium health insurance for all the people living below the poverty line. He suggests that medical colleges should teach their students to develop sensitivity towards the suffering of patients. They also need to modify their treatment approach for the poor, who cannot afford expensive treatment.

The aim of medical education should be to facilitate the application of medical technology so as to provide the best care to the poor at the most affordable cost. Dr Sudarshan says that the greatest joy he experienced was when he resuscitated a patient whose lungs and heart had stopped. He is also overjoyed when he sees the smiles on the faces of poor patients who leave the hospital with good vision after a cataract surgery. The country needs thousands of Dr Sudarshans to provide better health to our rural citizens.

Where Science and Spirituality Walk Together

Address to the European Parliament, Strasbourg, France

25 April 2007

Religion has two components, theology and spirituality. Theology is unique to most religions and the spiritual component is what spreads the values that human beings need to inculcate in themselves to promote a good human life and the welfare of society, while pursuing a material life. I would like to share an experience of how religion and science came together in a big mission.

I was fortunate to work with Prof. Vikram Sarabhai, the founder of the Indian space research programme, for about eight years. In the early 1960s, Prof. Sarabhai, with his team, had located a place technically most suited for space research after considering many alternatives. The place, called Thumba in Kerala, was selected for space research as it was near the magnetic equator, ideally suited for ionospheric and electrojet research in the upper atmosphere.

The major challenge Prof. Sarabhai faced was getting space in a specific area. As was normal, Prof. Sarabhai approached the Kerala government administrators first. After seeing the profile of the land and the sea coast, the view expressed was that thousands of fisherfolk lived there and the place had an ancient St Mary Magdalene Church, Bishop's House and a school. Hence, it would be very difficult to give this land, but they were willing to provide land in an alternative area. Similarly, the political powers also opined that it would be a difficult situation due to the existence of important institutions and the concern for people who were to be relocated. However, it was suggested that Prof. Sarabhai approach the only person who could advise and help. That was Rev. Father Peter Bernard Pereira, who was bishop for the region.

Prof. Sarabhai approached the Reverend on a Saturday evening, I still remember. The meeting between the two turned out to be historical. Many of us witnessed the event. Rev. Pereira exclaimed, 'Oh Vikram, you are asking for my children's abode, my abode and God's abode. How is it possible?' However, both men had the rare ability to smile even in tough situations. Rev. Pereira asked Prof. Sarabhai to come to church on Sunday at 9 a.m. Prof. Sarabhai went to the church with his team on Sunday. At that time Rev. Pereira was reciting passages from the Bible for Mass. After Mass was over, the Reverend invited Prof. Sarabhai to the dais. The

Rev. Father introduced him to the people. 'Dear children, here is a scientist, Prof. Vikram Sarabhai. What do sciences do? All of us experience, including this church, the light from electricity. I am able to talk to you through the mike which is made possible by technology. The diagnosis and treatment to patients by doctors comes from medical sciences. Science, through technology, enhances the comfort and quality of human life. What do I do, as a preacher? I pray for you, for your well-being, for your peace.

'In short, what Vikram is doing and what I am doing is the same: both science and spirituality seek the Almighty's blessings for human prosperity in body and mind. Dear children, Vikram says he will build, within a year, near the coast, alternative facilities to what we have. Now, children, can we give your abode, can we give my abode, can we give God's abode for a great scientific mission?' There was total silence, pin-drop silence. Then, every single person in the church stood up and said, 'Amen', making the whole building reverberate.

That was the church where we had our design centre, where we started rocket assembly, and the Bishop's house was our scientists' workspace. Later the Thumba Equatorial Rocket Launching Station led to the establishment of the Vikram Sarabhai Space Centre and space activities transformed into multiple space centres throughout the country. Now this church has become an important centre of learning, where thousands of people learn about the dynamic history of India's space programme and the great minds of a scientist and a spiritual leader. Of course, the citizens of Thumba got well-equipped facilities, a place of worship and an educational centre in an alternative place at the right time.

When I think of this event, I can see how enlightened spiritual and scientific leaders can converge to revere human life. Prof. Sarabhai is no longer among us; Rev. Pereira is not among us either, but those who are responsible for creation and making flowers blossom will themselves be a different kind of flower as described in the Bhagavad Gita: 'See the flower, how generously it distributes perfume and honey. It gives to all, gives freely of its love. When its work is done, it falls away quietly.'

Try to be like the flower, unassuming despite all its qualities.

Going Green

Address to the students participating in the Vaho Viswamitri Abhiyan, Vadodara

10 August 2013

A clean home leads to a clean nation. How? A clean home leads to clean streets and roads. Clean streets and roads lead to clean villages and towns. Clean villages and towns make clean districts and finally a clean state. A clean state leads to a clean nation. Wherever you are, whatever you do, you can certainly make a difference to the environment. It could be at home, school or college or it could be at work or even walking on the road or in the garden. Let me tell you a story about the evolution of a green environment.

Two decades ago, I was working at the Defence Research and Development Organization (DRDO), where I had the responsibility of setting up missile ranges and developing the long-range missile AGNI. One of the missile ranges was in

Chandipur, Orissa. Chandipur is a beautiful place against the background of the seashore. I have always been happy to see the sea, since I was born and raised on an island. At Chandipur, despite the beauty of the seashore, I always felt that something was missing because the whole missile range looked barren. Wherever possible, hundreds of trees were planted. But because it was a big area, even that was insufficient and the area still looked barren. How to make Chandipur green became the challenge.

In May 1989, the missile range at Chandipur was very busy. The countdown to the launch of AGNI-I had us working around the clock for many, many days. We had a number of technical problems and faced several geopolitical pressures, leading to anxiety in the scientific community and political circles. On the day of the launch, all the top guns had landed at Chandipur, and joined my technical team. While the countdown to the next morning's launch was in progress, the defence minister K.C. Pant, Dr Arunachalam (Scientific Advisor to Raksha Mantri) and I were walking on the beautiful seashore near the missile range. It was a full-moon night. Our anxieties for the launch at Chandipur turned into positive thinking. The defence minister was discussing what would come after the AGNI-I launch.

Suddenly, while we were walking, the defence minister turned to me and said, 'Kalam, I am sure that tomorrow's AGNI-I launch will be successful. What would you like to have from me?' I was stumped, not knowing what to ask for. Spontaneously, because of what was playing in my subconscious mind, I blurted out, 'Sir, can you sanction the planting and growing of 1,00,000 trees for the Chandipur missile range?' There was pin-drop silence. The minister said, 'What a beautiful request. I will sanction as many trees as you want.'

Today, the Chandipur range, full of trees, looks beautiful. With the budget allocated, we were also able to create an artificial lake, using groundwater and rainwater. Today, this lake has become a place of attraction, since birds from many parts of the world come here during the winter. I always cherish this incident of planting 1,00,000 trees and creating an artificial lake, because I consider it one of the most beautiful events in my life. Of course, subsequently the AGNI-I launch gave birth to an island missile range full of trees and with turtles in the background. On the island, apart from the large number of plants and trees, we can see a large number of turtles laying eggs in the isolated area. With the protected environment in our island ranges, it is a great sight to see turtles hatching from the eggs and baby turtles reaching the sea.

The Indian Navy—A Silent Force

Address to army officers, families and students of the Army School and Kendriya Vidyalaya, Jabalpur

11 July 2011

I would like to share with you a few thoughts on the topic 'My Flag is My Life'. From 2002 to 2007, I was the Supreme Commander of the armed forces. In that capacity, I was always keen to know the environment in which our armed forces operate, their state of readiness, their problems and challenges.

On 13 February 2006, I took a ride underwater in the naval submarine, *INS Sindhurakshak*. I entered the submarine through the lower lid of the conning tower and descended for about ten metres. The submarine dove to a depth of about thirty metres from the surface and started cruising. Through a narrow circular door of one metre in diameter, I entered the submarine control room. The crew explained the functioning of the submarine, demonstrating the manoeuvring operations and buoyancy control methodologies with great enthusiasm. It was a thrilling experience for me to cruise with the Chief of Naval Staff and the young sailors and officers. During the review, I was shown the underwater communication system, target identification and launch simulation. This was followed by the firing of a torpedo or a missile to simulate an attack, demonstrating the combat capability of our underwater silent force. The target location, signature analysis from the sonar data, torpedo launch and its homing were presented. I realized the complexities involved in underwater warfare.

I moved on to the weapon storage compartment where the torpedoes are stored; this compartment connects to the front of the submarine where water is filled before launching the torpedoes. Then I moved through various compartments to the rear of the submarine to see the diesel engine-based propulsion system and the electric drives. I met ninety officers and sailors in the vessel, all working like busybees. Their job was not easy but they were proud of their challenging mission. We went to a small working room where seven people could be accommodated. We had a delicious vegetarian lunch. I was given a presentation on future submarine building plans for the next thirty years.

The submarine, after completing its underwater journey of three hours, was ready to surface. The procedure started and the vessel came to the surface and moved in the direction of the shore. I climbed up through the ladder of the conning tower. I saw the land and the ocean behind me. What a memorable underwater journey. Our navy is indeed multi-dimensional—under water, on the water and above the water. The high morale shown by the sailors and the officers in the submarine is commendable and inspiring.

A Land of Ancient Time

Address at the launch of Hinduism: An Introduction *at the Akshardham Temple, New Delhi*

1 July 2011

The presiding deity at the Rameswaram Temple is a Shiva lingam, called Ramanatha, and it is one of the twelve jyotirlingas. I am tempted to say a few words about Rameswaram, since I was born and brought up there and I have a strong umbilical connectivity to Rameswaram even today. It is where my ninety-four-year-old brother lives with family, including his great-great-grandchildren. My brother is an integral part of the society of Rameswaram.

The great story associated with Rameswaram is a part of the great Indian epic Ramayana. Even though the great war fought by Rama that resulted in the destruction of Ravana and the return of Sita was based on high dharmic principles, the great Rama was guilty of killing an accomplished Vedic scholar, Ravana. This was a sin that brings out the importance Hinduism gives Vedic scholarship. To purify himself from the sin of killing Ravana, Rama had to perform a special puja for Lord Shiva. Rama requested Hanuman to get a Shiva lingam. Hanuman, with his characteristic greatness, went to Kailash and fetched two lingams from Shiva himself. But there was a hitch. The puja was to be performed in a predetermined auspicious time. Since Hanuman's return from Kailash was delayed, Sita made a lingam out of sand there, and the puja was performed at the auspicious time. When Hanuman came back with two beautiful lingams from Shiva himself, he saw that Rama had already completed the puja. He was angry and tried to remove the sand lingam and replace it with the divine lingams.

But even the great might of Hanuman could not move the seemingly fragile sand lingam from its position. Soon Hanuman was tired and sad. Rama told Hanuman that even though they had finished the puja that day, in the future, everybody could worship the two lingams he had brought first and only then perform the puja to the Ramalingam, the one installed by Sita and Rama. This tradition in Rameswaram continues even today.

This story teaches us that even Purushottama, the Supreme Being, is not absolved of his actions against a scholar. It also stresses the importance of time, and the nobility and humility of a leader.

A Culture of Beauty

Samvatsar Lecture at the Sahitya Akademi, New Delhi

16 February 2011

I am of the view that whatever the educational pursuits of a young person may be, humanities and literature must be a part of the curriculum. The interpretation of literature in our life experience is continuous. Literature enriches the mind eternally.

In 2005, while I was the President of India, I visited the north-eastern states of Sikkim, Assam, Meghalaya and Mizoram. I had the occasion to meet many literary personalities and thinkers working in north-eastern languages. They have contributed many literary works and cultural programmes to society. I was moved to see a unique musical and dance performance in Mizoram. Also, in Sikkim, I saw a fusion of the cultures of three groups of people, namely, Nepali, Bhutia and Lepcha, in that integrated society. The music and dance was so powerful and beautiful that all of us were very happy to see the unity of minds and how these different cultures came together when the normal practice in society seems to be the projection of prevalent differences.

Something happened in Mizoram that reflects the cultural ethos of the region. Normally, no aircraft takes off from Aizawl, the capital of Mizoram, after 4 p.m. Since I had work in Aizawl until 9 p.m. and had to return to Delhi that very night, the Indian Air Force organized my departure from Aizawl at that late hour, with certain temporary night-time take-off facilities. I reached the airport with my team, where we were joined by the minister and other officials. I saw an impressive scene unfolding in the midst of darkness with only the aircraft lights on. Near the aircraft and at a safe distance, a choir was in attendance with musical instruments. As soon as they saw me, they sang a lovely farewell song composed by a Mizo poet, Rukunga. The poem is titled 'The World of Parting'.

Now we part with heavy and painful heart,
The world we live in has been destined for parting,
By the heavenly father above
But we are destined for a better world than this
A city eternal, where we will never know painful partings

I was touched by the emotional content of the tune, the cultural diversity and unity of minds in this vast land of ours and the literary power of the author.

A Few Good Men

Address at the first lecture series on the occasion of the 50th National Maritime Day Celebrations, Goa

10 December 2012

When I was standing at the Pietermaritzburg railway station, my thoughts were hovering on two events that I had experienced in South Africa. One memory was from Robben island where Dr Nelson Mandela had been imprisoned for twenty-six years, in a very small cell, and the other was from his house.

Cape Town is famous for its Table Mountain; it has three peaks, called Table Peak, Devil Peak and Fake Peak. It is a beautiful sight throughout the day, sometimes covered with dark clouds and sometimes with white clouds embracing the peaks. Table Mountain is very close to the Atlantic coast and I flew by helicopter to Robben island from Cape Town in ten minutes. When we reached the island, except for the roar of the sea, the whole island was silent, symbolizing one thought: this is the place where the freedom of individuals was chained. Ahmed Kathrada, a South African, who was imprisoned at the same time as Dr Mandela, received us at the island.

What surprised me was the condition of the room where sleeping and all other human needs had to be fulfilled. It must be remembered that Dr Mandela, who is six feet tall, was imprisoned in that room for twenty-six years, fighting apartheid. The major part of his life was spent on this silent island. He used to be taken to work in a quarry in the nearby mountain for a few hours every day, in the bright sun. In time, his sight was damaged. In spite of his body being tortured he revealed to the world his indomitable spirit. This was the time he wrote a manuscript of freedom in tiny letters every day, when the jail wardens went to sleep. This tiny lettered manuscript finally became his famous book, *A Long Walk to Freedom*.

It was a great honour for me to meet Dr Mandela in his house in Johannesburg. What a moving reception the eight-six-year-old man, who was all smiles, gave me. When I entered Dr Nelson Mandela's house, I saw the cheerful face of the mighty man who freed South Africa from the tyranny of apartheid. When I was leaving from his house he came to the portico to see me off and, while walking, he discarded his walking stick and I became his support.

I asked him, 'Dr Mandela, can you please tell me about the pioneers of the anti-apartheid movement in South Africa?' He responded spontaneously. 'Of course. One of the great pioneers of South Africa's freedom movement was

M.K. Gandhi. India gave us M.K. Gandhi, we gave you back Mahatma Gandhi after two decades. Mahatma Gandhi was an apostle of non-violence.'

That is indeed the tradition of India, to enrich whichever nation we go to—it is almost our foremost responsibility. Enriching the nation is not limited to simply economic terms but it also means enriching the nation with knowledge, with sweat and, above all, with honour and dignity.

Happiness of the Whole

Address at and interaction with Kendra Vidyalaya students on the occasion of the golden jubilee celebrations of the Kendriya Vidyalaya Sangathan, Chennai

11 December 2013

I was climbing towards the top of the Acropolis in Athens when I came across a group of 150 Greek students. They threw a spontaneous smile at me; the teachers came forward and introduced the students. They said they were very happy to see the Indian President and that the children would like to hear a few words from him. I was, at that time, thinking about the great personalities the land of Greece had given to the world: Socrates, Plato and Aristotle. The words of Plato were ringing in my mind when I saw the young students. 2400 years ago, Plato in Book IV of *The Republic* states that 'our aim in founding the state was not the disproportionate happiness of any one class, but the greatest happiness of the whole'. Similarly, around the same period the Tamil poet-saint Thiruvalluvar said:

The important elements that constitute a nation are: being disease free, high earning capacity, high productivity, harmonious living and strong defence.

We have to find how we can provide all these elements to the citizens of every nation on an equitable basis for happiness for all.

With these thoughts, I made up my mind about what to say to the students and the youth of Greece. I slowly repeated, line by line, a hymn that I normally hear in Indian spiritual centres.

Righteousness

Where there is righteousness in the heart,
There is beauty in the character.
When there is beauty in the character,
There is harmony in the home.
When there is harmony in the home,
There is order in the nation.
When there is order in the nation,
There is peace in the world.

When the students and the youth repeated these words with me, the other tourists at the Acropolis also repeated them and there was applause all around. Then I realized how people from multiple nations, both young and experienced, were influenced by the thought of righteousness in the heart irrespective of their nationality. You can see how righteousness in the heart generates beauty in the character of human beings and beauty in the character leads to harmony in the home. Harmony in the home in an integrated way generates order in the nation. Of course, order in the nation finally blossoms into peace in the world. Righteousness in the heart is the starting point for a great individual, great family and great nation and ultimately a great planet Earth.

A Tiny Island

Address to and interaction with DRDO scientists and staff, Balasore

5 January 2012

I would like to share a personal experience that occurred in October 1993, when the development of the Prithvi missile was almost over. The army wanted to conduct a confirmatory test, on a land range, to validate Circular Error Probability. Our efforts to conduct the tests in the desert range could not take off due to range safety problems. To overcome this, we were looking for an uninhabited island on the eastern coast to conduct the tests.

On the hydrographic map supplied by the navy, we saw a few islands in the Bay of Bengal off Dhamra (Orissa coast) indicating that there was some land mass. Our range team, consisting of Dr S.K. Salwan and Dr V.K. Saraswat, hired a boat from Dhamra and went in search of the island. On the map, these islands were marked as Long Wheeler, Coconut Wheeler and Small Wheeler. The team carried a directional compass and proceeded on the journey. However, they lost their way and could not locate the Wheeler islands. Fortunately, they met a few fishing boats and asked them for the route. The fishermen did not know about the Wheeler islands but they said there was an island called Chandrachood. They thought that this could be the Wheeler island. They gave approximate directions for proceeding to Chandrachood. With this help the team reached the Chandrachood island, which was later confirmed as the Small Wheeler island. By this time it was late in the evening and it was dark.

The boatman refused to take us back in the night and the team had to stay in the Small Wheeler island in the boat for the night. The next morning, the team came back to Dhamra. On a physical survey of the three islands, we found that the Long Wheeler island had eroded over a period of time and was not useful for range activities. In view of this, we chose Small Wheeler, which had the adequate width and length required for range operations. After taking over the islands from the Orissa government for range activities, this one tiny island has been transformed into a world-class island missile range complex by our DRDO team.

The team also found some signs of occupation by other countries for the purposes of fishing. Also, they noticed a flag flying on Small Wheeler. I bring up this point for the reason that the Andaman and Nicobar islands also have many uninhabited islands which are close to many other countries. It is essential to have continuous surveillance of unauthorized activities on our uninhabited islands.

A Foundation of Tolerance

Address at the Gandhi Jayanti celebrations at the Sringeri Centre, Toronto, Canada

26 September 2010

At the end of August in the year 1947, Gandhiji happened to be in Bengal when communal violence broke out in the region including Calcutta. The violence was flaring up despite the deployment of a huge number of law enforcement forces. On 1 September alone, more than fifty people were killed in communal clashes. That night, Gandhiji went on a fast.

A follower questioned Gandhiji about the rationality of the decision and asked him, 'How can you fast against the hooligans?'

Gandhiji replied, 'If I falter now, the conflagrations may spread quickly. I can almost guarantee that two or three foreign powers will be upon us and try to end our short-lived dream of independence.'

He began his fast on 2 September and within a day, hundreds of violent demonstrators began coming to him and laying down their arms. The city witnessed many processions of peace in which people from all the communities participated. Gandhiji, who was then seventy-seven years old, fasted for three days, and brought lasting peace and order to the state of Bengal while other parts of the nation were still in communal turmoil. Lord Mountbatten, the outgoing British Viceroy of India, remarked that 'one unarmed man had been more effective than a force of 50,000 troops'.

Gandhiji was the greatest champion of peace and tolerance for all humanity. His life and ideals are relevant even today, perhaps more so globally than ever before, as we find ourselves in a world where people and ideas flow rapidly across national boundaries. Tolerance will have to become the foundation for a sustainable and secure future.

A World without Borders

Keynote address at the 20th International Economic Convention, 2012, at R.D. National College & W.A. Science College, Mumbai

9 December 2012

One day, when I was travelling in an aircraft in the US, I was told that much of its controls were software driven with a high likelihood of the software being developed in India. When I presented my credit card, I was told that it was being processed in the back-end server located in Mauritius. When I walked into a multinational software company in Bangalore, I was fascinated to find that it truly presented a multicultural environment.

A software developer from China, a software engineer from India and a hardware architect from the US were working together under a project leader along with a communication expert from Germany with a goal of solving a banking problem in Australia.

A.P.J. Abdul Kalam

When I see people working together like one family forgetting about the culture they come from or the language they speak, I feel that the only hope for such borderless interaction to continue is to inculcate the spirit of 'borderlessness' in every human activity on our planet Earth.

Serving Silently

Address at the inauguration of the National Conference on 'Declining Interest in Science Education and Research Among Students: Reasons and Remedies', Hyderabad

29 March 2013

I have known Mr M.B. Verma for the last two decades and he comes from the Darbhanga district. He studied in Darbhanga and Patna and reached the very senior position of Project Director, Light Combat Aircraft (Aeronautical Development Agency, Bangalore), working with state-of-the-art supersonic fighter aircraft. This is a boy who came from a very small village in Bihar and made a success of himself. Although Mr Verma worked for many decades in Bangalore, when the time came for him to retire, he decided to settle down in his home district and work for the people of Bihar.

Normally, people who work in big cities will choose to settle down in the big cities only. Today, Mr Verma is responsible for rural science education through three mobile science laboratories. The three mobile laboratories have spontaneously attracted students, even teachers, to perform scientific experiments. How many of you would like to settle down in your home village, after retirement, like Mr Verma?

The Thoughts of a Boy

Address to the students of Journalism and Communication at the Makhanlal Chaturvedi University of Journalism and Communication, Bhopal

12 December 2012

In October 2010, I visited Bhopal, where I had an appointment with about ten children from the Sohagpur rural block of Hoshangabad district in Madhya Pradesh, about 150 kilometres from Bhopal. The appointment was for 9 p.m., but because my flight was delayed, the meeting could begin only at 11.30 p.m. These children, mostly tribal and all from government schools in villages, had a very special initiative which they ran in the form of a monthly newspaper called '*Bachchon ki Pahal*', entirely managed by a group of about 250 child reporters, all under the age of fifteen.

They showed me many different editions of the newspaper, which were all very unique. In each of the editions, these young dynamic and fearless reporters brought forth local issues of concern, the state of schools and village community areas, highlighted the latest trends in technology and science and even interviewed local officials, including the district magistrate, about the progress on local developmental activities. One very unique column they carry in each edition is geared towards the preservation of traditional tribal words. It is a commendable effort by the younger generation to protect their traditions and is relevant to us all.

In my interaction with them they asked me many questions, one of which I would like to share with all of you. One young fourteen-year-old child reporter, Gopal, asked me, 'Dr Kalam, you told us about the right to free and compulsory education and how it would bring access to education to all children. But I want to ask you, how can a child from a nomadic community, that constantly keeps moving from one place to another, pursue education in mainstream schools?' It was a brilliant question to which I replied that the need of the hour is to evolve mobile schools where education in their own language can follow the child. I would like all of you to evolve a strategy for addressing the problem highlighted by our young reporter, Gopal.

I visualize a scenario where children speaking different languages are brought together at a common interaction platform of knowledge. How can a child from Tamil Nadu and a child from Hoshangabad and another child from Kashmir all be propagators of their local information, and learn from each other? How do we bridge the language barriers in school education? We must also give thought to how we can help to connect children across the nation and preserve the local languages of the nation.

I am sharing this unique experience of 'Bachchon ki Pahal' from the tribal youth to the university. The university and you future media-persons may like to encourage this type of reporting of these important issues. The university can organize a state meet of all young writers, who are interested in local-and village-level culture, problems and progress.

Write on a Page

Address to and interaction with the students of Radha Govind Group of Institutions, Meerut

6 March 2014

What would you like to be remembered for? You have to evolve yourself and shape your life. You should write it on a page. That page may be a very important page in the book of human history. And you will be remembered for creating that one page in the history of the nation.

Lessons for Life

'Born in a fisherman's family, he lived through poverty and worked during his school and college days to become an outstanding aeronautical scientist and later the President of India. His life will be an inspiration for all the Indian people, particularly the younger generation.'

D. Raja, Communist Party of India

A Gift is a Dangerous Thing

Address at the PepsiCo Annual Operations Conference, New Delhi

22 February 2014

This was an incident that occurred just after India became independent and I was in still in school. Rameswaram was a beautiful place with a population of 30,000 people. My father was elected president of the Rameswaram Panchayat Board. One day, I was studying in my house when I heard a knock at the door. We never used to lock our door in Rameswaram in those days. A stranger opened the door, came in and asked me where my father was. I told him that Father had gone for evening namaz. Then he said, 'I have brought something for him, can I leave it here?'

Since my father had gone to pray, I shouted for my mother to get her permission to receive the item. Since she was also reading namaz, there was no response. I asked the person to leave the item on the cot. After he left, I continued to study. After some time, my father arrived and saw a *tambalum* kept on the cot. He asked me, 'What is this? Who gave it?'

I told him, 'Somebody came and left this for you'.

He opened the cover of the *tambalum* and found there was a costly dhoti, *angavastram*, silver vessels, some fruits and sweets. He could see the note that the person had left behind. He became upset at the sight of the *tambalum* and gifts left by the stranger. I was his youngest child—he really loved me and I also loved him a lot. That was the first time I saw him angry and it was also the first time I got a thorough beating from him. I was frightened and started weeping. My mother embraced and consoled me. Then my father came and touched my shoulder lovingly and advised me not to receive any gifts again without his permission. He quoted an Islamic Hadith, which states that, 'When the Almighty appoints a person to a position, He takes care of his provision. If a person takes anything beyond that, it is an illegal gain.'

He then told me that this is not a good habit. Gifts are always accompanied by some purpose, so a gift is a dangerous thing. It is like touching a snake and getting poison in turn. This lesson stands out in my mind even now when I am in my eighties. This incident taught me a very valuable lesson for the rest of my life—it is deeply embedded in my mind.

I am sharing this thought with all of you, since I believe that one should not get carried away by a gift which is given with a purpose and through which one loses one's personality.

Manusmriti states: 'By accepting gifts, the divine light in a person gets extinguished'. Manu warns every individual against accepting gifts for the reason that it places the acceptor under an obligation in favour of the person who gave the gift. Ultimately, it results in making a person do things that are not permitted by law. And living within the law is the foundation of a good life.

Work with Integrity and Succeed with Integrity

'Dynamics of Creative Leadership', an address to and interaction with the students of Rajiv Gandhi Institute of Management (RGIIM), Shillong

25 June 2013

In 2010, I visited Mussoorie and interacted with the 85th foundation batch of newly inducted civil service officers and also addressed the Mid-Career Civil Services Officers Trainees (those who have eighteen years of service). I talked to the civil service officers about creative and innovative leadership and the evolution of a better world. After the session, the participants raised some unique questions, which highlight the opportunities and challenges that the nation's highest level of bureaucracy faces in governance.

My India: Ideas for the Future

I asked the young officers to ask themselves how they can be creative leaders who can pioneer great missions in life. After the lecture, one young lady officer got up and asked me, 'Dr Kalam, the bureaucracy is trained and known for maintaining the status quo. In this context, how can I be creative and innovative?' Another young officer said, 'Sir, right now, at the start of our service, we are all ethically upright and resolute with integrity. We all want to work hard and make a change. But, in a decade's time, in spite of my surroundings, how do I still maintain the same values with the same enthusiasm?'

To these questions, I replied that the young officers entering into governance have to determine a long-term goal for which they will be remembered. This goal will inspire them at all times during their career and help them overcome all problems. I told them that the young bureaucrats of the nation have to remember that when they take on difficult missions, there will be problems. Problems should not become our captain; we have to defeat them and succeed.

Another young officer asked me, 'Dr Kalam, you just administered an oath to us, "I work with integrity and succeed with integrity". But the political system and seniors who are corrupt would definitely put pressure on young bureaucrats to compromise their ethical standards. How can we tackle this problem?'

I thought about this problem, which is very pertinent and practical. I responded recalling my own experience where I worked very closely with politicians and administrators including in positions like Secretary of the Defence Research and Development Organisation, Scientific Advisor to Raksha Mantri, Principal Scientific Advisor to the Government of India. In all these positions, I was in charge of large missions with huge capital investments. At no point do I recall any leaders or administrators approaching me for favours.

Then I told the young officers that they can definitely establish a brand of integrity for themselves which will keep away those who want them to make ethical compromises. Of course, this may mean facing some problems in individual growth. Nevertheless, despite obstacles, the best traits in human beings will succeed in life.

A Nobel Winner

First Dr Ida Scudder Memorial Oration, Vellore

10 August 2012

Let us study the challenges faced by Marie Curie. She was not afraid of problems; she overcame all the obstacles she faced and succeeded. Her experience is definitely an inspiration for all of us. Marie Curie was a co-worker of Antoine Henri Becquerel's during his research and she discovered the properties of the element uranium. She came to know about those properties and set about investigating their effect, which she named 'radioactivity' for her doctoral research.

Marie Curie investigated many other elements to determine whether they too were radioactive. She found one other element, thorium, and also came across a source of radiation in a mixture called 'pitch-blend', a source that is much more powerful than either thorium or uranium.

Working together, it took Curie and her husband, Pierre, four years to isolate the radioactive source in the pitch-blend. Curie used to carry large quantities of pitch-blend on her head to extract the few grams of material that the laboratory needed. Those few grams of the material were her discovery. Curie named it radium. For the discovery of radium, Marie and Pierre won a Nobel Prize in Physics in 1903, which they shared with their friend Antoine Henri Becquerel. Shortly after, Curie found that what she had discovered was not pure radium but she was able to isolate the element itself after quite a struggle. For this work, she was given the Nobel Prize for Chemistry in 1911.

During her work, Curie discovered radiation could kill human cells. She reasoned that if it could kill healthy human cells, it could kill diseased human cells also and went about isolating radium for use in killing and treating tumours. During World War I, she went to work for the French, designing and building X-ray machines. Knowing that moving soldiers to a hospital before surgery was not always possible, she designed the first mobile X-ray machine and travelled with it along the front lines during the war.

On 4 July 1934, Curie died in Paris, killed by her own experiments. She died of radiation poisoning and may have been the first person to do so. Curie had brought herself up from poverty, struggling to finish her education and succeeding brilliantly. The work she did, she did with patience, often getting results only after years of careful experimentation, while struggling for money to support her work. For her struggles, she received two Nobel Prizes, becoming the first woman to win even one. Through the knowledge she gained, thousands of lives have been saved. The courage and perseverance Madame Curie showed in the pursuit of her scientific mission are indeed remarkable and stimulating.

No Time for Fear

Address to the Air Force officers and staff, Air Force Administrative Staff College, Coimbatore

19 February 2012

On 8 June 2006, I flew in a Sukhoi Su-30 fighter plane to understand how a sortie was undertaken in a combat aircraft. The previous night, Wing Commander Ajay Rathore had given me lessons on how to fly. He was my friend and teacher who successfully taught me how to pilot the plane as well as handle the fighter's weapon control system. Flying a fighter aircraft had been a dream for me since 1958 when I became an engineer. After our strapping in, the Sukhoi took off and soared to a height of 25,000 feet, flying at a speed of over 1200 kilometres per hour. Wing Commander Rathore suggested that I turn the craft to the left and then to the right. I experienced gravitational forces of about 3g, of course wearing a g-suit.

I could feel the banking of the Sukhoi to the left and right going up and down before landing.

During the sortie, I tried to understand various subsystems integrated into the aircraft, all developed by Indian scientists. I was very happy to see the indigenously built mission computers, radar warning receivers, IFF (Identification Friend or Foe) and display processors in the aircraft. I was also shown how to locate a target in the air and on the ground with the help of synthetic aperture radar. The flight lasted for over thirty minutes. I experienced the fulfilment of a great aim and long-cherished dream of my life. Above all, I realized the leadership qualities of the air warriors who are engaged in the defence of our national airspace.

As soon as I landed, a number of reporters surrounded me, asking questions. One asked, 'You have flown an aircraft at this age? Weren't you scared?' I immediately replied, 'Since I was busy understanding the working of the subsystems and manoeuvring the flight with the pilot, I didn't have time to let fear into my mind.'

When we are deeply involved in our work and we love our work, there is no question of fear overpowering us.

The Price of a Book

Samvatsar Lecture of the Sahitya Akademi, New Delhi

16 February 2011

I was studying at the Madras Institute of Technology, Chrompet, Chennai, from 1954 to 1957. It was perhaps in the second year of my course, in December 1955, when all my classmates were away for the winter vacation. But I had not prepared well for one subject and decided to remain in the hostel and prepare for my forthcoming exam. During this vacation, one day I got a trunk call from my brother-in-law, Ahmed Jalal, saying that Rameswaram had been severely hit by a cyclone and my parents wanted to see me immediately. I too wanted to go to Rameswaram to look after my parents and home.

It was the end of the month and I was left with no money. There was also no time for my family to send the money. I was wondering what I should do to arrange for the money to travel. I had only one item of value with me at that time: the precious book presented to me by Dr Lakshmanaswami Mudaliar, for my excellent performance in aerodynamics during my second year. The book was *The Theory of Elasticity* by Timoshenko and Goodier and cost Rs 400 at that time. It was a very difficult decision for me to sell a book that was a prize for my performance. But since I needed a minimum of Rs 60 to go home, I took the electric train from Chrompet and reached Moore Market near Central Station.

In those days, Moore Market was the place where one could buy old or new books at a very reasonable cost. I had earlier purchased a second-hand copy of *Light from Many Lamps* for just Rs 20 and it had become a guiding light for my life. The bookstall where I purchased *Light from Many Lamps* was run by a pious Brahmin with a traditional tuft. I approached him and told him that I had a book and needed to sell it, so that I could get enough money for this emergency trip home. He told me to show him the book and asked me how much money I needed. I told him I needed at least Rs 60, though I felt he would give me much less.

He opened the book and read the first page and found that it was a prize given to me by the then vice chancellor of Madras University. He immediately told me that he was not going to buy the book. I was worried that I may not get any money. Then he told me that since the book was a present from Dr Lakshmanaswami Mudaliar, he was going to give me Rs 60. He would keep the book with him till I came back and returned the money. I was very happy that one soul was trying to help me in a difficult situation and also understood my interest in studies.

I got the money and went to Rameswaram only to see nature's fury, but all my thoughts were on getting the book back. As soon as I returned from Rameswaram, I went to Moore Market, paid the money and got the book back from the noble shopkeeper as promised. After that I was happy; I felt like a mother seeing her son who had been lost for some time. Books always give us knowledge, but in times of need, they can also become wealth.

A Transparent Movement

Address to and interaction with the students of Nirmala Convent School, Bulandshahr

17 December 2012

On 21 November 2005, I visited Adichunchanagiri Math, attended a function of FUREC (Foundation for Unity of Religions and Enlightened Citizenship) and interacted with over 54,000 students from various schools and colleges in Karnataka. There, a tenth standard student, M. Bhavani from Adichunchanagiri Composite High School, Sharavathy Nagar, Shimoga, asked me the following question:

'Sir, I would like to live in a corruption-free India. Please tell me, Dr Kalam, what can young people like me do to contribute towards removing corruption?'

The agony of young minds is reflected in this question and for me it was an important question. I thought about the kind of solutions we could have.

There are one billion people in the country and nearly 200 million homes. In general, there are good citizens everywhere. However, if we find that the people in a few million houses are not transparent and not amenable to the laws of the country, what can we do? These homes have, apart from the parents, one or two children. If these parents are deviating from the transparent path, the children can use the tools of love and affection and correct their parents and bring them back to the right path.

I asked all the children assembled in that gathering, 'What would you do if your parents deviated from transparency? Will you boldly tell them, father or mother, that they are not doing the right thing, the things that you were taught by them and in school?' Most of the children spontaneously responded, 'We will do it!' They are confident because they have love as a tool. I have also asked parents, in other meetings, what they would do if asked to return to transparency by their child. At first there was silence; later, many of them hesitantly agreed that they would abide by the children's suggestion since it is driven by love. They made me an oath. Can you now repeat it with me?

'I will lead an honest life free from all corruption and will set an example for others to adopt a transparent way of life.'

I call upon all of you today, to start a movement to create transparency at home. I am convinced that the ignited mind of the youth is the most powerful resource on the earth, above the earth and under the earth. You can make a change at home.

A Fast for a Cause

Address at the first lecture series on the occasion of the 50th National Maritime Day Celebrations, Goa

10 December 2012

I had a unique experience a few years ago that reveals how a single leader can inspire a large population. I happened to meet Mahatma Gandhi's granddaughter, Mrs Sumitra Kulkarni, in Delhi. She told me a story about her grandfather, which she personally witnessed.

Each day, as you are aware, Mahatma Gandhi used to hold a prayer meeting at a fixed time in the evening. After the prayers there would be a collection of voluntary monetary gifts for Harijan welfare. Gandhjii's followers used to collect whatever the people of all sections of society donated and hand it over to the Gandhi family's supporting staff for counting. Gandhiji would be told how much it was before dinner. The next day, a bank official would come to collect this money. On one occasion, the official reported that there was a discrepancy of a few paise between the money given to him and the money collected. Gandhiji, on hearing this, went on a fast, saying that it was a donation for the poor and they must account for every paisa. His act of righteousness should be practised by all of us. On this day, as managers and leaders of tomorrow all of you must dedicate yourselves to practising righteousness in all your thoughts and actions.

The Social Media Phenomenon

Address to the employees of the New Indian Express, *Bangalore*

31 August 2012

Yesterday, while I was on the flight from Delhi to Bangalore, I read a book called *Cognitive Surplus*. In the book, the author, Clay Shirky, says that 'social production' is increasingly become relevant today. He calls this 'commons-based peer production', or work that is jointly owned or accessed by its participants, and created by people operating as peers, without a managerial hierarchy. The inclusion of millions of new participants in our media environment has expanded the scale and scope of such production dramatically.

Earlier people spent many hours watching TV. Today things are changing. Free time is termed as 'cognitive surplus' in the book. Free time is being used in a different way today than in earlier times. The book states that 'for the first time in the history of the medium, young people are watching less TV than their elders, turning away from passive consumption of TV towards active participation'. There is a paradigm shift happening today from TV to social media. The Indian media has to take cognizance of this fact and consider how it will take shape in a new dynamic situation.

About six months ago, I also joined the social networking space with my official page, www.facebook.com/officialkalam. I also launched the electronic version of the e-journal Billion Beats, www.facebook.com/kalambillionbeats. My official page, which my team and I update and manage every day, now has about 1.2 million subscribed members and a reach of over 2.5 million users. I have been regularly sharing real-life events and ideas on this page, which the users comment on and interact with. Of the hundreds of posts that I have put up on it, two posts have specifically attracted people. Let me share them with you.

The first is a post about a young boy with courage. I was in Harali village in Maharashtra where I met 2000 students from different schools. Just as I was about to descend from the stage, a young boy, about eighteen years of age, held in his mother's arms, cried out to meet me. I called them both on the stage. The boy could not walk due to some childhood disease but his will was strong.

He told me, 'My name is Shailesh and I am from this village. You told me to have a dream. I am here to tell you my dream. I am a chess player . . . and some day I will become a Grand Master.'

My India: Ideas for the Future

I told all my Facebook friends that it was great to see such aspirations and strength in a rural boy who, despite his challenges, has a great goal. People responded to the post and many of them wished to support and help Shailesh realize his dreams. The post was commented on and liked by over 50,000 people within one day.

The second post was about an experience I had when travelling in Uttar Pradesh. After visiting a healthcare inauguration in Azamgarh, I was travelling on the state highway towards Varanasi airport with my team when I spotted this roadside tea stall. We suddenly stopped the convoy for some tea and samosas. I was impressed by the quality of service, food and how all this was managed by a single man who was the owner, cashier, cleaner, tea maker and server, all in one. I told my Facebook subscribers, 'Let me tell you, there is no place which can match tea at an India roadside chai shop . . . How do we encourage and standardize such entrepreneurs which bring taste to our nation?' Tens of thousands of people shared this post and commented with their ideas to promote such local entrepreneurs at the grassroots level.

One lesson which comes from these comments and this user viewership pattern on my Facebook page is the way that the citizens want positive and interactive news. They are looking for stories of success and hope. They are eager to participate in the process of changing the lives of others and changing the nation through their action. The media, in all forms, needs to gear up to meet these twenty-first century expectations of the youth of the nation.

The Heart of an Engineer

Address to and interaction with the participants at a seminar, 'Science for the Welfare of Mankind', De Paul International Residential School, Mysore

29 June 2010

Sir M. Visvesvaraya was a great person, who etched for himself a permanent place in the hearts of Indians by his engineering talent, public service and honesty. Yes, I am referring to Sir Mokshagundam Visvesvaraya, who is a household name in the country.

He was born on 15 September 1860 in Muddenahalli, Chikkaballapur taluka, Karnataka, and distinguished himself as an eminent Indian engineer and statesman with his talent and human qualities over a life spanning 101 years. Every year, 15 September is celebrated as Engineer's Day in India in his memory. He was awarded the Indian Republic's highest civilian honour, the Bharat Ratna, in 1955. He was also knighted by the British for his contributions to the public good. The young Visvesvaraya lost his father at the age of fifteen. He attended primary school in Chikkaballapur and high school in Bangalore. He earned his BA from Madras University in 1881 and later studied civil engineering at the College of Science, Pune, now known as the College of Engineering, Pune.

Upon graduating as an engineer, Visvesvaraya took up a job with the Bombay Public Works Department and was later invited to join the Indian Irrigation Commission. He implemented an extremely intricate system of irrigation in the Deccan area. He also designed and patented a system of automatic weir water floodgates which were first installed in 1903 at the Khadakvasla reservoir near Pune.

Visvesvaraya designed a flood protection system to protect the city of Hyderabad from floods. He supervised the construction, from concept to inauguration, of the Krishna Raja Sagara dam across the Cauvery river. This dam created the biggest reservoir in Asia at the time it was built. Visvesvaraya was rightly called the 'Father of the modern Mysore state' (now Karnataka). He was responsible for building the very first electricity generation plant in Asia at Shivanasamudra near Mysore in 1894. In 1908, Visvesvaraya was appointed Diwan or First Minister of the princely state of Mysore. He was responsible for founding many industries and educational institutions. He was also known for his sincerity, time management and dedication to many causes.

Visvesvaraya led a very simple life. Before accepting the position of Diwan of Mysore, he invited all his relatives to dinner. He told them very clearly that he would accept the prestigious office on the condition that none of them would approach him for favours. He introduced compulsory education in the state—something that was later embodied as a fundamental right in the Constitution of independent India. Sir Visvesvaraya belongs to that small band of eminent Indians whose ideas and achievements along with certain cherished value systems have been among the truly creative and formative forces of modern India.

Young Helpers

Interaction with the students of Presidency School, Bangalore

29 August 2010

Nagappan, Sathiyan and a dozen other young students used to celebrate their birthday parties in hotels and enjoy lavish dinners. Suddenly, four years ago, Nagappan and his friends decided not to spend money for their birthdays in hotels. Instead, they chose to pool the money to help underprivileged students.

A physically disabled junior student hailing from a very poor family was the first beneficiary of their gesture and was able to pay his college fees. The smile on the face of the poor disabled boy motivated Nagappan and others to mobilize more students who were willing to contribute around twenty to twenty-five rupees every month. The entire amount collected was pooled for supporting the education of more such poor and disabled students.

The encouragement from their fellow students inspired Nagappan and Sathiyan to form a trust called Young Helping Minds. Soon, they registered the trust deed with the relevant authorities and also with the Income Tax Department.

Today, they are proud of the 250 students and young people who contribute a small share towards the noble cause of educating poor and disabled children. The organization currently supports thirty-five such students but wants to increase the number of contributors to 1000 and the number of beneficiaries to 100. This is a unique and wonderful model that has come out of the imagination of a few students.

A Long Way from Poverty

Address at the graduation day of the J.N.N Institute of Engineering, Chennai

14 June 2013

Mario Capecchi had a difficult and challenging childhood. For nearly four years, Capecchi lived with his mother in a chalet in the Italian Alps. When the Second World War broke out, his mother, along with other Bohemians, was sent to the Dachau concentration camp as a political prisoner. Anticipating her arrest by the Gestapo (the official secret police of Nazi Germany), she sold all her possessions and gave the money to friends to help raise her son in their farm. In the farm, Capecchi had to grow wheat, harvest it and take it to the miller to be ground. However, the money which his mother had left for him ran out and at the age of four and a half years, he was left to fend for himself.

He started living in the streets—sometimes joining gangs of other homeless children, sometimes living in orphanages and most of the time hungry. He spent a last year in the city of Reggio Emelia, hospitalized for malnutrition, where his mother found him on his ninth birthday after a year of searching. Within weeks, Capecchi and his mother sailed to America to join his uncle and aunt.

Capecchi started his third grade schooling afresh. Later, he studied political science but didn't find it interesting and changed to science to become a mathematics graduate in 1961 with a double major in physics and chemistry. Although he really liked physics and its elegance and simplicity, he switched to molecular biology in graduate school on the advice of James D. Watson, a co-discoverer of the structure of DNA.

Capecchi's objective was to do gene targeting. He started his experiments in 1980 and by 1984, he had clear success. Three years later, he applied the technology to mice. In 1989, he developed the first mice with targeted mutations. The technology created by Capecchi allows researchers today to create specific gene mutations anywhere they choose in the genetic code of a mouse. By manipulating gene sequences in this way, researchers are able to mimic human disease conditions on animal subjects.

What the research of Mario Capecchi means for human health is nothing short of amazing. His work with mice may lead to a cure for Alzheimer's disease or maybe even cancer. His innovations in genetics won him the Nobel Prize in 2007.

The Duty of a Scientist

Address to students at the Khalifa University of Science, Technology and Research, Sharjah, UAE

6 November 2013

C.V. Raman was among the first set of people to be awarded the Bharat Ratna, India's highest civilian honour. The award ceremony was to take place in the last week of January, shortly after the Republic Day celebrations of 1954. The then President, Dr Rajendra Prasad, wrote to Raman inviting him to be his personal guest at Rashtrapati Bhavan for the award ceremony. Raman wrote a polite letter, regretting his inability to be present. He had a noble reason for his inability to attend the investiture ceremony. He explained to the President that he was guiding a PhD student and that the thesis was positively due by the last day of January. The student was valiantly trying to wrap it all up and Raman felt he had to be by his student's side, see that the thesis was finished, sign the thesis as the guide and then have it submitted.

Here was a scientist who gave up the pomp of a glittering ceremony associated with the highest honour, because he felt that his duty required him to be by the side of the research student. It is this scholarly approach that truly builds science. It is indeed a message to research guides and teachers.

An Indomitable Spirit

Interaction with the students of Presidency School, Bangalore

29 August 2010

I would like to recall the great clarion call given by C.V. Raman, at the age of eighty-two—to always have an indomitable spirit. The message still reverberates in my mind: 'I would like to tell the young men and women before me not to lose hope and courage. Success can only come to you by courageous devotion to the task lying in front of you. I can assert without fear of contradiction that the quality of the Indian mind is equal to the quality of any Teutonic, Nordic or Anglo-Saxon mind.

'What we lack is perhaps courage; what we lack is perhaps a driving force, which can take one anywhere. We have, I think, developed an inferiority complex. I think what is needed in India today is the destruction of that defeatist spirit. We need a spirit of victory, a spirit that will carry us to our rightful place under the sun, a spirit that will recognize that we, as inheritors of a proud civilization, are entitled to a rightful place on this planet. If that indomitable spirit were to arise, nothing could hold us from achieving our rightful destiny.'

Knowledge is equal to the equation: Knowledge = creativity + righteousness + courage + indomitable spirit.

Dream Your Dreams

'Kalam taught us how to dream big, without the fear of winning or losing. He continues to live in our hearts. Above all, he showed the world he was a simple man with big dreams. Let us strive to make this world a better place to live in and aim for success of an India he dreamt of.'

N. Chandrababu Naidu, Chief Minister of Andhra Pradesh

How I Found My Wings

Address to the teachers of the School and Mass Education Department, Bhubaneswar

January 2014

When I think of my childhood days, I am reminded of Sivasubramania Iyer, who taught me when I was in the fifth standard, at the age of ten. He was a great teacher in our school. All of us loved to attend his class and listen to him. One day, he was teaching us about the flight of birds. He drew a diagram of a bird on the blackboard, showing the wings, tail and the body with the head. He explained how birds create lift and then fly. He also explained to us how they change direction while flying. He spoke for nearly twenty-five minutes, telling us about lift, drag, how birds fly in a formation of ten, twenty or thirty.

At the end of the class, he wanted to know whether we understood how birds fly. I said I did not, and so the teacher asked the other students whether they had understood or not. Many students said that they had also not understood. Our response did not upset him, since he was a committed teacher.

Mr Iyer then said that he would take us all to the seashore. That evening, the whole class went to the seashore in Rameswaram. We enjoyed the roaring waves knocking at the sandy hills in the pleasant evening. Birds were flying, chirping in sweet voices. He pointed out the seabirds in formations of ten to twenty. We saw the marvellous formations of birds, moving with a purpose and we were all amazed. He asked us to pay attention to what they looked like when they were flying. We saw their wings flapping. He directed us to look at the tail and the combination of flapping wings and twisting tail. We looked closely and noticed that the birds used that mechanism to fly in the direction they desired.

Then he asked us a question: 'Where is the engine and how is it powered?' Birds are powered by their own lives and the motivation of what they want. All these aspects were explained to us in fifteen minutes and we all understood the dynamics of bird flight from this practical example. How nice it was! Our teacher was a great teacher; he could give us a theoretical lesson coupled with a live practical example from nature. This, I feel, is real teaching.

For me, it was not merely an understanding of how a bird flies. The bird's flight entered into me and created a special feeling within. From that evening onwards, I decided that my future studies had be in flight and flight systems. My teacher's teaching and the event that I witnessed decided my future career. Then one evening, after classes, I asked the teacher, 'Sir, please tell me how to progress further in learning all about flight.' He patiently explained to me that I should complete my eighth-standard studies and then go to high school. He suggested that I should thereafter go to engineering college, where I could study flight. If I completed all my education with excellence, I might do something connected with flight sciences. This advice, along with the exercise he showed us, gave me a goal and a mission for the rest of my life. When I went to college, I studied physics. When I went on to study engineering at the Madras Institute of Technology, I specialized in aeronautical engineering.

Thus my life was transformed into that of a rocket engineer, aerospace engineer and technologist. That one instance of my teacher giving us an interesting lesson and then showing us a live example proved to be the turning point in my life that eventually shaped my profession.

The Power of Young Minds

Address at the inauguration of the Aerospace Festival 2013, Tanjore

21 January 2013

In 2005, I participated in the award ceremony of Shankar's International Children Competition at New Delhi. There I encountered thirteen-year-old Aardhra Krishna's vision of how civilization on Earth would look around 3000 CE. In her imagination, the people of Earth have been forced to migrate to Mars and have built a flourishing civilization. This advanced civilization is suddenly threatened by an asteroid from Jupiter, whose orbit is approaching Mars, putting the planet in danger of extinction. The scientists on Mars come up with the very innovative plan of firing a barrage of nuclear cannons at the oncoming asteroid.

The bombardment destroys the asteroid and the year 3000 sees an Earth-Martian civilization surviving the fury of nature using an innovative scientific application. What wonderful scientific and technological thinking from a young mind! I was so impressed! Aardhra Krishna got the first prize. While I was admiring the imagination of this young student, a real time-space experiment took place that gave some meaning to the imagination of the youth.

On 4 July 2005, the NASA spacecraft *Deep Impact* crashed into the comet Tempel 1 with enough force to create a football-stadium-sized crater with the depth of a fourteen-storey building. The spacecraft was steered through a ground control system managed by Shyam Bhaskaran. *Deep Impact* travelled 431 million kilometres in 172 days, escaping from Earth's orbit to intercept the comet at a straight distance of 134 million kilometres from Earth. The comet was orbiting around the Sun every five and a half years. This was a landmark in radio communications and space exploration and an important milestone in the development of standardized techniques to combat asteroids, which may hit Earth in the future.

The second incident I would like to narrate to you occurred on Friday, 21 September 2007, while I was at the Jet Propulsion Laboratory (JPL) in Pasadena, USA, and visited the Mars rover prototype laboratory. A young lady, Jenny, explained the features of the Mars rover being developed in detail. After that impressive presentation, the deputy director of JPL told me about the young professional. As an eighth grader, the young lady had developed an interest in Mars. She went on to study mechanical engineering.

During this period, like many other students, she was also working in a famous restaurant, which was usually very crowded. She used to meet a couple regularly and impressed them with her approach to her job. They asked her, 'Are you going to continue in this job as your career?' She replied, 'Definitely not. I have my eyes set on a Mars exploration.' A few days later, on an extremely busy day for her in the restaurant, the same couple was there and they called her over and introduced her to a group from JPL. She was extremely excited and told them about her dream. Very soon, she got a call and was offered a job in JPL, working in the Mars robotic lab. Her joy knew no bounds. She was extremely happy to be a part of the Mars rover development team.

These two incidents reveal how powerful ignited minds can be. The ignited mind of a youth is the most powerful resource on the Earth, above the Earth and under the Earth.

Make the Impossible Possible

Address at the 11th National Book Fair, Lucknow

27 September 2013

I would like to share with you a real-life story, which happened two decades ago in Honolulu. I read about this incident in the book *Everyday Greatness* written by Stephen R. Covey.

Geri and Lindy Kunishima had two daughters, Trudi, thirteen, and Jennifer, nine, and a young son, Steven. At the age of eighteen months, Geri detected something abnormal in his son, Steven. A CT scan revealed that Steven's vermis, an area of the brain that transmits messages to and from the body's muscles, had not developed. The neurologist told them that Steven would never walk or talk, and that he was profoundly disabled. Geri couldn't eat or sleep for days. Seeing her father's sadness, Trudi challenged the doctor's prognosis and announced that she did not believe what the doctor said about Steven. She took an oath that she would work with her mother till Steven became normal. They started reading a passage to him every day at the dinner table, which soon became a habit. Jennifer and Trudi also asked Steven questions and pointed out to him animals or people illustrated in the books. For many weeks there was no response from Steven.

After three months, one evening, Steven suddenly wriggled away from the cushions. The family watched him inching towards the children's books. Steven grabbed a book, flipped through it till he saw the page filled with pictures of animals. The following night, as Jennifer prepared to read to him, her brother crawled to the same book and opened the same page again. This showed that Steven had developed memory, which continuously improved.

Both Trudi and Jennifer played the piano in Steven's presence. One day, after practising, Jennifer lifted Steven from his place under the piano. He was making a new sound. He was humming the music! The family also worked to build Steven's muscles through a massage school. Geri, Trudi and Jennifer dabbed peanut butter on the boy's lips; by licking it off, he exercised his tongue and jaw. When Steven was four and a half years old, he still couldn't speak words, but he could make 'aaah' and 'waaah' sounds and he had a remarkable memory. After studying a 300-piece jigsaw puzzle, he could assemble the pieces in one sitting.

After many rejections, Steven was admitted to preschool, to the Robert Allen Montessori School by the then director,

My India: Ideas for the Future

Louise Bogart, who found that Steven was determined to make himself understood.

One day, Bogart stood off to the side and was watching the teacher work with another child on numbers. 'What number comes next?' the teacher asked. The child drew a blank. 'Twenty!' Steven blurted out. Bogart's head turned. Steven had not only spoken clearly but had also given the correct answer.

Bogart approached the teacher. 'Did Steven ever work on this?' she asked.

'No,' the teacher answered. 'We worked with him a lot on numbers one through ten. But we didn't know he had learned any beyond ten.' Bogart told Steven's mother about this incident. 'This is just the beginning of what Steven is capable of,' she said.

His motor skills remained poor, so Jennifer, Geri and Trudi worked hard at making his written scrawl legible. 'I can do it.' Steven assured Jennifer one day. 'Just give me time'. After that, Steven continuously improved and was admitted to a mainstream Catholic school in 1990.

Such is the power of collective determination to cure a child and make the impossible completely possible.

A Master of Arts

Address at the inauguration of the education seminar on the 125th consecration of the Aruvippuram Siva Temple, Neyyatinkara

28 January 2013

On 19 November I received a very interesting visit at home. It was an eighty-eight-year-old woman with her daughter, a professor at Jawaharlal Nehru University, and her son-in-law, a journalist. She told me about her ambitions and her struggle in an orthodox family to get a graduate degree. But her formal education was only until the fifth standard. This lady's name is Sethu Ramaswamy. She gave me a book titled *Bride at Ten, Mother at Fifteen* that she had written. Marriage, intensive family commitments, children, grandchildren, great-grandchildren and her family circumstances did not allow her to fulfil her ambition to become a graduate. The quest for knowledge kept her dreaming that one day, she would become a postgraduate. She was married to a freelance journalist at the age of ten and became a mother at the age of fifteen. In the book, she says, 'All my life, like countless Indian housewives, I was an unknown woman—a woman of no consequence. But at the age of eighty, I became a known Indian woman—a person of some consequence. What had I achieved in my life until that point? I had brought up six daughters, the first being born when I was fifteen, the last when I was twenty-nine.'

This is the saga of a woman who has lived in two countries and seen her own family make the transition from tradition to modernity. She has seen the ups and downs of life while bringing up her daughters. I was astonished to get to know this indomitable spirit. She finally fulfilled her life's dream at the age of eighty. She had worked, worked and worked while taking care of her daughters' children as well. Despite all her family commitments, she was proud to announce everywhere that she was pursuing an MA degree, at the age of seventy-eight, through distance education, from Annamalai University through the Delhi Centre. When she passed the MA examination, she proudly said, 'I passed my MA and my degree came by post. It was a bare second division but I have at last fulfilled a great desire, my life's ambition that was burning within me.' The message we derive from this is:

Age doesn't matter; if you have a great aim in life, you can achieve, achieve and achieve.

I Can Do It

Address to students and teachers, Chandrapur

14 February 2014

When I met the tribal students of Lead India 2020 at Rashtrapati Bhavan, I asked all of them one question: 'What do you want to become?' Out of many responses, there was one from a visually challenged boy studying in the ninth standard. His name was Srikanth and he said, 'I will become the first visually challenged President of India.' I was very happy to see his vision and ambition because I feel that a small aim is a crime. I congratulated him on realizing what his vision was and told him to work towards achieving this vision.

Thereafter, he worked hard and got 90 per cent in the tenth standard and 96 per cent in intermediate, and he set himself the goal of studying engineering at the Massachusetts Institute of Technology, Boston, USA. His relentless hard work meant that he not only secured the seat, but he got a full fee waiver. The training he received under the initiative of Lead India 2020 has set high aspirations for him. Seeing the impact of this training, the Lead India 2020 movement and General Electric (GE) volunteers have funded Srikanth's travel to the US. When GE offered him a job on graduating, he told them that he would certainly come back to GE if he couldn't become the President of India. What confidence that boy has amidst the difficulties and challenges in his life as someone who is visually challenged!

Recently, when I met physically challenged students at a meet organized by the Government of Tamil Nadu and Lead India 2020 at Coimbatore, I had the chance to meet Srikanth and his teacher. Srikanth is in the fourth year of his degree in Computer Science and Management. In these four years, he has started a company that produces consumer-packaging items using biodegradable materials. He has also started a social initiative that provides skill development training to the youth. He gave an inspiring extempore speech on how to overcome disability and how having a strong mind and will power will help you overcome challenges and succeed.

The message here is that it doesn't matter who you are—if you have a vision and determination to achieve that vision, you will certainly achieve it.

The Shoemaker's Son

Address at the Bharatiya Temple and Cultural Centre, Kentucky, USA

11 April 2010

Lincoln was born in the state of Kentucky in February 1809. He lost his mother when he was ten years old. He lived with his father in Indiana in the woods, which had many wild animals. Lincoln had only eighteen months of formal schooling and he was largely self-educated. He made extraordinary efforts to attain knowledge while working on a farm, splitting rails for fences and keeping a store at New Salem, Illinois.

Lincoln was a captain in the Black Hawk war, spent eight years in the Illinois legislature and rode the circuit of courts for many years. His law partner said of him, 'His ambition was a little engine that knew no rest.' In 1858, Lincoln ran against Stephen A. Douglas for senator. He lost the election but in his debates with Douglas, he gained a national reputation that won him the Republican nomination for President in 1860.

As President, he rallied most of the northern Democrats to the Union cause. On 1 January 1863, he issued the Emancipation Proclamation that declared the slaves within the Confederacy free forever. Lincoln is remembered for this great action.

Bourgeois, a very arrogant man, stood up before Lincoln gave his maiden address to the Senate. He said, 'Mr Lincoln, before you start I would like you to remember that you are a shoemaker's son.' And the whole Senate laughed. They couldn't defeat him but they could humiliate him. But it is difficult to humiliate a man like Lincoln.

Lincoln said to Bourgeois, 'I am tremendously grateful that you reminded me of my dead father. I will always remember your advice. I know that I can never be as great a president as my father was a shoemaker.' There was utter silence because of the way Lincoln had chosen to respond to the comment.

And then he said to Bourgeois, 'As far as I know, my father used to make shoes for your family too. If your shoes are pinching or you have some trouble—although I am not a great shoemaker, I learned the art from my very childhood—I can fix them. And I would say the same to anybody in the Senate: if my father has made your shoes, and if they need any correction, any improvement, I am always available. Although one thing is certain, I can't be as good. His touch was golden.'

And tears came to his eyes at the memory of his great father. Of course, some senators cried too.

This incident brings out the humility of a great leader and is a lesson for all humanity.

Learn to Fly

Address at the Jammu Students Meet, Jammu

3 February 2014

In December 2011, I was in a village called Paravur near Kochi. I went to the village to inaugurate the Sasthrayaan Programme for the propagation of science education. During the programme, the President of the Paravur Panchayat Board and the local MLA said that the mission of the Sasthrayaan Programme was to prepare 2000 students from different schools for entrance exams so that they could become engineers, scientists, doctors, managers and civil service officers. This would empower 2000 families of the village. My inaugural address to the Paravur audience of 5000 students and family members was entitled 'Science Empowers the Nation'.

After my speech, hundreds of hands went up to ask questions. Because I was short of time, I selected twelve students randomly to ask me questions. I would like to share with you two questions of concern asked by the students. One girl in the tenth standard asked me, 'Sir, next year I have to choose a subject for my specialization. I love psychology. However, my parents do not agree. They want me to take a subject that will enable me to enter a professional course. What should be my choice?'

I thought about it and then I told the girl, 'You have a great tool to win your parents over: love and affection for them. Similarly, your parents also love you. They earn and sometimes also borrow money for your education. They would like to ensure that you are properly positioned in your professional life. But I respect your dream and I am confident that you can persuade your parents. If you need any additional help, I also can talk to your parents.'

Fortunately, the girl's parents were also present, in the parents' enclosure. They got up and said, 'We are the parents of the girl who daringly asked the question. We love our child. We will definitely go ahead and support her wish to take up psychology as her choice of subject.' The whole audience cheered both the parents and the young girl.

The next important question was from a boy from the eighth standard who had come from a faraway village to the city. He was nervous and represented the youth in Indian villages. The boy started by telling me his name. 'My name is Vishnu. I don't know what I should ask. I am nervous. I have not asked any questions in class. I need to have confidence; I have not gained confidence through education over the past seven years. I am afraid to talk to my teachers; I am afraid to talk to my friends. Whenever I talk, I compare myself with other students in their elegant clothes. Please tell me, Dr Kalam, how can I become a unique person? I want to become a marine engineer. I want to travel in ships. I want to be the captain of a ship. I want to build the engine for the ship. Will I be able to do all this, Dr Kalam? How can I achieve this mission? What should I do?'

When the boy completed the question, the whole audience of 5000 people and dignitaries on the dais, including the chief minister, who was present, was looking at me, wondering what I was going to say to such a sincere question from a young boy from a village. I thought about it for a long time. I wanted to break the silence. I said, 'My dear Vishnu, you have put to me the most difficult question I have received so far from the millions and millions of students whom I have met. Vishnu, I value your question; I also think you are echoing the question of millions of rural students.'

Then, slowly, I gained the confidence to answer. 'Let us both recite a beautiful poem titled "I Will Fly".' I slowly started the poem and Vishnu started repeating the poem with me:

I Will Fly

I am born with potential.
I am born with goodness and trust.
I am born with ideas and dreams.
I am born with greatness.

A.P.J. Abdul Kalam

I am born with confidence.
I am born with wings.
I am not meant for crawling.
I have wings, I will fly.
I will fly and fly.

When Vishnu finished reciting the poem, he was in tears. He said, 'I have gained confidence—I will win, I will win and win.' and went back to his seat.

Out of the World

Address at the felicitation programme for Dr K. Radhakrishnan, Chairman, Indian Space Research Organisation (ISRO), Irinjalakuda

29 January 2010

Picture a boy. A simple boy, about ten years old, walking with his parents on this soil; he is a pious boy worshipping at the famous Koodalmanikyam Temple with his parents; he is a creative boy going to Kathakali classes to learn this beautiful dance from Kerala; he is a sincere boy regularly going to National High School and graduating from Christ College. That boy grew up with a mind full of questions. That boy was none other than Dr Koppillil Radhakrishnan, the chairman of ISRO, a space research organization that has put India on the map of spacefaring nations. Today he leads both ISRO—with a unique culture and more than

14,000 dedicated ISRO-ites—and India to be at the top spot in space research.

Now, just like me, all of you in the audience, particularly the youth of Irinjalakuda, must be wondering if Radhakrishnan ever knew when he was a young boy, when he was going to school or to college, that he would one day become the chairman of ISRO. Only Dr Radhakrishnan can answer this question. But let me try and imagine how he attained the prestigious position of the chairman of ISRO.

As a young boy, when he saw the height of the temple, when he saw the great coconut trees of Irinjalakuda; when he saw the twin rivers of his hometown; when he heard his teachers giving examples of great human beings in life, a real seed was sown in his young mind. When he was learning Kathakali, the epic heroes must have inspired him; certain books that he read as a young boy could have elevated his mind. Against this background, the young Radhakrishnan would have certainly had a vision. He would have dreamt: 'I want to fly—I want to fly like any of my big city friends to reach great heights in life.' And, of course, the legacy of his ancestors, who were in the teaching profession, might also have contributed.

Radhakrishnan grew up with an aim and was flying with the great goal and continuously acquiring knowledge. He came into contact with great minds, great teachers and great poets of Kerala, learnt about great engineers like Visvesvaraya, great scientists like C.V. Raman, great mathematicians like Srinivasa Ramanujan. Above all, he was also influenced by his family traditions, native culture and knowledge of Irinjalakuda. He acquired the habit of working hard, with devotion, from the environment around him. One of the most beautiful traits that any great scientist, any great technologist or, for that matter, any great leader should possess is perseverance.

What is perseverance? This quality is something we all learnt from a famous chairman of ISRO, Prof. Satish Dhawan. He indeed defined perseverance: When you want to achieve, when you want to become a great leader, when you are involved in a great mission, you are aware that there will always be problems. A leader never allows a problem to be his or her captain; he becomes the captain of the problem, defeats the problem and succeeds.

As the leader of ISRO, Dr Radhakrishnan prepares himself for the challenges of the future. One thing is certain; The atmosphere that Irinjalakuda, with the Koodalmanikyam Temple devoted to Bharatha—a symbol of dharma and idealism and the spiritual bridge of multiple faiths—gave him and the guidance his early teachers gave him will definitely add strength to his approach. To this he adds the quality of perseverance from his research guide, Prof. Satish Dhawan. A fortuitous combination of these unique traits and his environment has shaped Dr Radhakrishnan. And so, remember that dreams transform into thoughts, thoughts result in action and knowledge makes you great.

Mind Over Matter

Address to and interaction with children during the 40th anniversary celebrations of Balavidyalaya (a school for deaf children), Chennai

12 February 2010

Pavithra Mukundan, the first child of Chitra and Mukundan Nair, was born in October 1985—one month premature. Immediately after birth, Pavithra was found to have a congenital cardiac problem. She underwent a heart surgery for patent ductus arteriosus when she was ninety days old. When she was one year old, her parents suspected she had a hearing impairment. After consulting her paediatrician, they met ENT surgeons who put them on to audiologists. After several visits, she was diagnosed with bilateral neurological hearing loss (severe to profound) and was fitted with hearing aids.

Pavithra had the symptoms of Rubella (German measles). It is likely that her mother had Rubella during her early pregnancy. As per the audiologist's recommendations, Pavithra joined Balavidyalaya's Early Intervention Programme in March 1987 when she was one year and five months old.

At Balavidyalaya, Pavithra wore pocket model hearing aids. It was very difficult to put the harness and the two hearing aids on a child who hardly weighed nine kilograms. Saraswathi Narayanaswamy was Pavithra's first teacher. Pavithra was found to be extremely intelligent, hard-working and well mannered and her parents were very cooperative and hard-working too. Initially, the child attended school for one hour a day and her mother also attended school along with the child. The mother was counselled and guided to accept the deafness in the child as a challenge and not the end of her dreams for her daughter.

Soon, her school hours were increased. Valli Annamalai and Mahalakshmi Sundaram joined the teaching team. Pavithra progressed fast and started developing basic listening skills. She could notice the presence and absence of sound, associate sounds with their source, distinguish sounds and comprehend what she heard. She started picking out objects when they were named, sorted marbles according to their colour and size, sorted blocks according to their shapes, threaded beads as per instructions. By the time Pavithra was two and a half, she was able to comprehend simple commands and short sentences. She enjoyed looking at picture books—she was a happy child and took part in all school activities.

At that stage, Pavithra was moved to the preschool and was introduced to activities that laid the foundations for reading, writing and number work. She started matching words with pictures, sentences with suitable pictures and fared well in all the exercises. She started talking fluently, answering questions and easily taking part in conversations. After completing the course in Balavidyalaya in April 1991, Pavithra was admitted to Chinmaya Vidyalaya, Chetpet, Chennai, in the first standard.

At the regular school, Pavithra's reading and writing skills were found to be way ahead of those of the unimpaired children in her class. Her progress in the school was smooth and she was one of the toppers in her class throughout. Her mother kept in close touch with her regular school as well as Balavidyalaya. Every time she had a question, she found answers from the staff of Balavidyalaya.

However, Pavithra continued to be underweight. She developed scoliosis and her spine developed a curve that became more pronounced after she was thirteen or fourteen years old. But Pavithra's spirits were always high. She continued to be cheerful and had many friends. Pavithra graduated from the tenth standard with a proficiency award and passed the twelfth-standard board examinations with good credentials. She did her BCom from Women's Christian College, Chennai. She enjoyed her college and joined the MSc programme (Information Science) at the University of Madras.

After graduation, she joined the Connemara Public Library in Egmore as a digital librarian. Later she shifted to

Everonn Systems, Chennai, as a library consultant. Pavithra stands as a symbol of self-confidence in spite of her hearing impairment and scoliosis. Balavidyalaya has succeeded in bringing special needs children into the mainstream and transforming them into a great asset to the nation.

Dreams of Steel

Convocation address at GEMS B School, Chennai

11 April 2011

It happened in 1893. A ship was sailing from Japan to the US. There were hundreds of people on that ship including two significant personalities, Swami Vivekananda and Jamsetji Tata. Swamiji asked Jamsetji what mission he was travelling for. Jamsetji said that he wanted to bring the steel industry to India. Swami Vivekananda blessed him. He suggested that steel technology had two components: steel science and material technology. 'What can you bring to this country in terms of material technology?' he asked. 'You will have to build material science within the country too.'

Jamsetji thought about it and then made a decision. He went to London and asked for technology transfer for a steel plant. The UK steel manufacturers looked at Jamsetji and said that if Indians made steel, the British would eat it. Jamsetji crossed the Atlantic Ocean, talked to the Americans and brought steel manufacturing technology to India. And Tata Steel was established in Jamshedpur. Jamsetji seeded and worked for the steel plant. He is not there now, but 10 million tonnes of steel per annum is rolled out of the plant. The visionary Jamsetji gave one portion of his assets to start a science institute that is today known as the Indian Institute of Science, in Bangalore.

The message I would like to convey is—dreams give you visions, visions give thoughts and thoughts lead to actions. Jamsetji brought two establishments to India—the first was a steel plant and the other an educational research institution based on the vision of Swami Vivekananda.

A visionary like Jamsetji, with the blessing of Swamiji, paved the way for the establishment of the Indian Institute of Science in 1909. This institute, born out of the vision of great minds, is the foremost scientific research institution in India, providing postgraduate education. This institution as envisaged by Swami Vivekananda, has one of the best material science labs, providing the best research results for the development and production of material for various research and development labs and industries. The Indian Institute of Science is also a renowned institution in various areas such as physics, aerospace technology, biology and biotechnology. This is one institution where different kinds of technologies, such as biotechnology, information technology and nanotechnology, converge. The results will have a tremendous influence on improving solar cell efficiency and healthcare, particularly on drug delivery systems.

Believe in Your Work

Address at the Children Science Congress, Thiruvananthapuram

4 January 2010

Galileo was born in Pisa, Italy, and was the first of the six children of Vincenzo Galilei, a famous music theorist, and Giulia Ammannati. Four of their six children survived infancy and the youngest, Michelangelo, became a noted composer.

Although Galileo seriously considered the priesthood as a young man, he enrolled for a medical degree at the University of Pisa at his father's urging. He did not complete this degree, and instead, studied mathematics. In 1589, he was appointed to the chair of mathematics in Pisa. In 1591, his father died and he was entrusted with the care of his younger brother, Michelangelo.

In 1592, he moved to the University of Padua, teaching geometry, mechanics and astronomy until 1610. During this period, Galileo made significant discoveries in both pure science and applied science. His multiple interests included the study of astrology which, in pre-modern disciplinary practice, was seen as being correlated to the study of mathematics and astronomy.

Galileo's discovery of the telescope and his first statement about the dynamics of our planets with respect to the Sun at that time was an important discovery. For that discovery, he was imprisoned, because people reacted with hate and dissent when he tried to convey that the Earth was motionless and not the centre of the world. The Earth, in fact, moved around the Sun.

Stephen Hawking says, 'Galileo, perhaps more than any other single person, was responsible for the birth of modern science.' Galileo's life gives two messages to children: they must pursue the subject for which they have a passion and work for the truth without any fear.

The Power of Positive Thinking

Address at the Maulana Azad Medical College Old Students Association, New Delhi

20 December 2012

Recently, I was reading a book about the life story of Morris Goodman, who is an author and international speaker. I was inspired to read about him and how the power of his mind alone resulted in a new life for him. Goodman was injured in an aeroplane accident on 10 March 1981 and was completely paralyzed. His spinal cord was crushed, the first and second cervical vertebrae were broken and his swallowing reflex was destroyed. He could not eat or drink and his diaphragm was destroyed. He could not breathe. All he could do was blink.

The doctors, of course, said that he would be a vegetable for the rest of his life. That is the picture they saw of him, but it did not matter what they thought.

The main thing was what Morris Goodman himself thought. He pictured himself being a normal person again, walking out of that hospital. He had to work within the hospital with his mind and he says, once you have your mind, you can put things back together again. He was hooked to a respirator and the doctor said he would never breathe on his own again. But a little voice kept telling him, breathe deeply, breathe deeply and finally he was weaned from it. The doctors were at a loss for an explanation. Goodman could not afford to allow anything to come into his mind that would distract him from his vision. He had set a goal to walk out of the hospital on Christmas and he did it. The doctors said it could not be done. He walked out of the hospital on his own two feet. That was a day he would never forget. The message Morris Goodman gives to the world in six words is: 'Man becomes what he thinks about.'

My Driver, the Doctor

Address at the Lucknow Literature Carnival, Lucknow

7 December 2013

I was in Madurai to inaugurate the Paediatric Oncology Cancer unit at Meenakshi Mission Hospital on 7 January 2011. When I completed the task, suddenly someone approached me; his face looked familiar. When he came closer to me, I found out that he used to be my driver during my Defence Research and Development Laboratory days at Hyderabad.

When I was working there I had a driver called V. Kathiresan, who worked with me day and night for nine years. During that time I always saw him reading books, newspapers and journals of substance during his free time. That dedication attracted me. I asked him a question, 'What makes you read during your leisure time?' He said that he had a son and daughter who asked him a lot of questions, which made him study and try to answer to the best of his ability.

I told him to study formally through the distance education mode and gave him some free time to attend the course and complete high school and then to apply for higher education. He took that as a challenge and kept on studying and acquiring skills and upgrading his educational qualification. He earned a BA (History), then an MA (History) and then he completed another MA (Political Science). He also completed the BEd and MEd degrees.

He worked with me till 1992 and then he registered for a PhD at the Manonmaniam Sundaranar University, which he received in 2001. He joined the Education Department of the Tamil Nadu government and served there for a number of years. Now, in 2010, he has become an Assistant Professor in the Government Arts College at Mellur near Madurai. Such commitment and dedication have helped him to acquire the right skills in his leisure time which, in turn, made his career progress rapidly and upgraded his livelihood.

The message is this: it doesn't matter who you are, if you have a vision and are determined to achieve that vision through the constant acquisition of knowledge, you will certainly realize your goals.

To Give Is to Gain

'Dr Kalam was a true leader, not just for being a successful and intellectual Indian President in tough times but being a true humanitarian in every sense. His work for various NGOs in India to help those who were less fortunate with a true commitment to make a difference really showed in his words and his actions.'

Sheela Murthy, Founder, Murthy Law Firm, USA

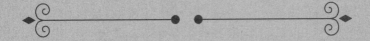

Service with Compassion

Address to and interaction with students of the University of Central Florida (UCF), Orlando, USA

27 September 2012

Sister Antonia Brenner lives in a prison cell in Mexico. In 1986, while working with a charity in Mexico, Aid for Baja California, Sister Antonia entered a prison for the first time. She was so profoundly affected that she was compelled to return, permanently and voluntarily. She begins each day with the prison roll call, which is not complete until her name has been called. Hers is not a nine-to-five job; she is on call twenty-four hours a day. She has the full run of the prison and walks about unescorted, serving the spiritual and practical needs of the over 2500 residents. If a prisoner needs a blanket or medical attention, needs words of praise and encouragement for a personal accomplishment or craves a warm hug, Sister Antonia makes sure that they get what they need.

Many things that seem inconsequential to most are miracles for the inmates, thanks to Sister Antonia. She intervenes with the system on their behalf. She visits their families, children and sick relatives, bringing them news from the outside. Sister Antonia is the 'mother figure' to all the male and female residents of the prison, helping them to see a future beyond the prison walls.

Sister Antonia has successfully started a hospice programme for inmates who are terminally ill. She says, 'People say to me that prisoners should lose their rights—this is the price they must pay for their crimes.' Her response: 'I say, lose their freedom, yes. But deny the positive power of love within a prison and you end up with only violent, vengeful energy.' She believes this evil energy can be channelled in a positive direction with people returning to society. She makes rehabilitation a reality, restoring self-respect. Sister Antonia asks for nothing, yet gives everything to make a difference in the lives of people most would rather forget.

There's a story I read about Sister Antonio in a book called *Everyday Greatness by Stephen R.Covey*, which highlights the need for leadership with compassion.

A riot was raging in La Mesa prison in Mexico. There were 2500 prisoners packed into a compound that had been built for only 600. They angrily hurled broken bottles at the police, who fired back with machine guns. Then came a startling sight. A tiny woman, five feet two inches tall and sixty-three years old, calmly entered the crowd with outstretched hands, in a simple gesture of peace. Ignoring the shower of bullets, she stood quietly and asked everyone to stop. Incredibly, the violent prisoners calmed down. No one else in the world but Sister Antonia could have done this. Why did the people listen to her? All because of her decades of voluntary service to the prisoners. She sacrificed all her life for the prisoners and lived amidst murderers, thieves and drug lords, all of whom she called her sons. She attended to their needs round the clock, procured antibiotics, distributed eyeglasses, washed bodies for burial and counselled the suicidal. These selfless acts of love and compassion commanded respect from the prisoners, making them control themselves and do what she wanted them to do.

What a great message for humanity! We have seen that there is a leader with compassion even for prisoners, but we need leaders with compassion for the voiceless millions in the world.

The Kidney Chain

Address at and interaction with members, students and JSS alumni, Maryland, USA

26 May 2013

I would like to share with you the noble actions of two human beings. One is a Christian missionary priest and the other is an industrialist. I got to know both while inaugurating the dialysis centre at the Kidney Federation of India in Thrissur, Kerala.

Rev. Father Davis Chiramel is from Perincherry, Kerala. Father Davis donated one of his kidneys to an electrician, Gopinathan, after he heard of his suffering through the media.

Kochouseph Chittilappilly is a well-known industrialist in the field of electrical equipment, construction and services in the state and the nation. In 2011, in a touching gesture of giving, Kochouseph Chittilappilly donated his kidney to an unknown ailing poor truck driver. This set in motion a unique movement called 'The Kidney Chain', wherein a relative of one patient would donate to another patient, whose relative would in turn donate to another and so on. Moreover, about 500 employees of his company pledged to donate their organs after death.

I told them that I was very happy to sit next to such great souls. I asked them, 'What made you give one part of your system and bear the suffering and pain you had to go through in the process? Above all, God has created two kidneys for a human being for some reason and you are not afraid to lose one of them? Please tell me how your mind and body cooperated in such a situation of physical agony to oneself to rid someone else of pain?'

Father Davis said only four words, 'It is God's wish.' Whereas my other friend Chittilappilly said, 'I am a well-to-do industrialist. And I have everything I need. I felt I should derive happiness from something I choose to do and God led me to the path of giving my kidney to an unknown truck driver.'

I studied both the givers in detail and wondered about the mental and physical pain they had to go through, the sense of fulfilment they had experienced after their suffering and the gift they freely gave—taking away the electrician and the truck driver's pain. I am sharing this experience that will make us realize that the human mind and body are highly complex and we are all integrated physiologically and psychologically and need to nurture both mind and body to live happily.

Six Virtues of a Healthcare Giver

Address at the graduation day of the Adichunchanagiri Institute of Medical Sciences, Mandya

22 March 2013

I would like to share an experience I had with Choakyi Nyima Rinpoche, the chief monk in Kathmandu and a medical researcher. After walking for nearly a kilometre, I reached the white Kumbha where the chief monk and his disciples were waiting to receive me. After the reception, Choakyi Nyima Rinpoche asked me to follow him to the study room. He climbed the first floor, the second floor, the third floor, the fourth floor and the fifth floor, just like a young boy. And all along, I kept walking behind him. When I finally reached his chamber, I saw a laboratory and a spectacular view of the Himalayas.

I was surprised to find out that the monk's research students come from different parts of the country. He introduced me to his co-author, David R. Shlim, MD, with whom he has written a book. Choakyi Nyima Rinpoche and I exchanged a few books, including the book David and he had co-authored. It was titled *Medicine and Compassion*. I liked this book and read it during my journey from Kathmandu to Delhi. This book lists six important virtues which a medical practitioner must possess in his or her attitude towards their patients.

The first virtue is generosity, the second is pure ethics, the third is tolerance, the fourth is perseverance, the fifth is cultivating pure concentration and the sixth is intelligence.

These virtues, I believe, will empower caregivers with a humane heart.

The Gift of Joy

Address at the Indo-American Community Programme, Virginia, USA

25 May 2013

The happiest moment of my life was a very unique experience. During my visit to a hospital in Hyderabad, I found many children were struggling to walk with an artificial limb (prosthetic) because it weighed over three kilograms. At the request of Prof. Prasad of the Nizam's Institute of Medical Science, the head of the orthopaedic department at that time, I asked my friends from my AGNI days why we could not use the composite material used in the AGNI heat shield to fabricate Floor Reaction Orthosis (FROs) prosthetics for polio-affected patients. They immediately said it was possible.

We worked on this project for some time and came up with an FRO prosthetic limb for children weighing around

300 grams instead of three kilograms, exactly one-tenth the weight the children were already carrying. The doctors helped us to fit the new prosthetic on the children and the children started walking, smiling and running around. With the lightweight device provided by the hospital they could run, ride a bicycle and do all sorts of things that they had been denied for a long time.

Their parents were overjoyed to see the happiness of their children. Tears rolled down their cheeks from the joy of seeing their daughters and sons running with light prosthetics. That is the moment which gave me bliss in my life above all other happy occasions.

A Heartening Story

Address at the Global Health Summit 2014, organized by the Association of American Physicians of Indian Origin, Ahmedabad

3 January 2014

In 2010, I had a beautiful experience while visiting Dr Sibu Saha's family in Kentucky. There I had a discussion with Dr Saha about his experiences as a cardiac surgeon. The human heart has two unique needs—one is that of kindness and the second is that the heart must function without any disorders. While I was at his home, Dr Saha narrated two cases—one dealing with a newborn child and the other related to a ninety-one-year-old person in Lexington.

The newborn baby had a congenital valve disorder, which meant there was restriction in the blood flow. The parents met Dr Saha with their child in the hope that somehow the child could be saved. As a young cardiac surgeon, it was a unique challenge for Dr Saha. With full confidence in his training and faith in God, he conducted the operation. The valve was rectified and the child was saved. The family was happy and the child became healthy again.

The second incident which Dr Saha narrated to me was indeed moving. This happened when Dr Saha had established himself as an experienced and renowned cardio-thoracic surgeon. One day, a ninety-one-year-old patient arrived at his clinic. The patient said that he was a pastor and his mission daily was to climb up fourteen steps to reach his altar and deliver his sermon. The pastor said that he could not climb even half the steps and was praying to God to help him recover from the problem. He had already seen two other surgeons who expressed their inability to help him due to his age. He wanted Dr Saha to help him 'recover his heart'.

Dr Saha concluded that the main artery valve was defective and had narrowed, thereby restricting the flow of blood. The question arose whether a major open-heart surgery should be conducted, given the patient's age. With this background, he met the patient and told him that it was going to be a major heart operation. The patient insisted that Dr Saha should go ahead and do whatever was needed to fully 'recover his heart'. With the blessings of God, Dr Saha operated on him and corrected the valve and got it working. And soon, the patient started recovering. Generally, such a surgery needs at least ten days of rest. The pastor, on the third day, said that he had to be in church the next day to deliver his Sunday sermon. The pastor went to the church, led the prayer and later came back to Dr Saha's care. In time, he recovered fully and went back to his pastoral service.

Here is a doctor who has a heart with a spirit of giving and with the skill of removing pain. Whether it is the heart of a newborn or that of the aged, God has given him all the grace and the medical expertise to give his patients a healthy life, irrespective of the age of the patients.

The Lady with the Lamp

Address at and interaction with the students of Holy Cross College, Tiruchirapalli

21 January 2013

When I think of how an individual can contribute to society, the story of Florence Nightingale, the mother of the nursing profession, comes alive in my memory. Florence Nightingale volunteered to work and care for thousands of wounded soldiers who were being shipped across the Black Sea to the military medical stations in Turkey. She walked four miles every night among sick soldiers with a lamp to light her way. The grateful soldiers would kiss her shadow as she passed by. She is definitely an example of the spirit of giving to remove the pain of suffering people. She opened the first nursing school and she wrote the first textbook of nursing in 1860. She inspired many women to take up nursing as a career. I particularly liked her thoughts on education. She said, 'Education is to teach not to know, but to do.'

Scientific Magnanimity

Address at and interaction with the Pavai Group of Institutions, Namakkal

3 October 2013

I would like to tell you about an incident that took place during the ceremony for awarding Nobel Laureate Prof. Norman E. Borlaug with the Dr M.S. Swaminathan Award. The ceremony was at Vigyan Bhavan, New Delhi, on 15 March 2005. Prof. Borlaug is a well-known agricultural scientist and a partner in India's first Green Revolution.

Prof. Borlaug, at the age of ninety-one, was being showered with praise by everybody gathered there. When his turn came to speak, he highlighted India's advancement in agricultural science and production and said that the political visionaries C. Subramaniam and Dr M.S. Swaminathan were the prime architects of the first Green Revolution in India. Even though Prof. Borlaug was himself a partner in the first Green Revolution, he did not speak of it. He recalled with pride Dr Verghese Kurien who ushered in the White Revolution in India.

And then came the real surprise! He turned to the scientists sitting in the third row, fifth row and eighth row of the audience. He identified Dr Raja Ram, a wheat specialist, Dr S.K. Vasal, a maize specialist, and Dr B.R. Barwale, a seed specialist. He said that all these scientists had contributed to India's and Asia's agricultural science. Prof. Borlaug introduced them to the audience by asking them to stand up and ensured that the audience cheered and greeted the scientists with great enthusiasm.

This was something I had never seen in our country before. I call Prof. Borlaug's action scientific magnanimity. If we aspire to achieve great missions in life, we need scientific magnanimity to help young achievers focus and grow. It is my experience that great minds and great hearts go together. Scientific magnanimity will motivate the scientific community and nurture team spirit. Experienced members of this community should cultivate the characteristics of value of science and scientific magnanimity, which will go a long way in motivating the youth to carry out quality research.

Where You Come From

Address at the 100th anniversary of Atash Adaran Fire Temple, Madras Parsi Zoroastrian Anjuman, Chennai

10 July 2010

Sir Jamsetji Jejeebhoy was one of the best-known and most illustrious sons of India, who rose from extreme poverty to fame and glory. Jamsetji spent his early years in Navsari playing with the children in his neighbourhood, his parents being unable to afford to send him to even primary school. After their death, he went to live and work with his maternal uncle in 1799. There, he taught himself elementary accounting and a smattering of English. Jamsetji made five voyages to China and back, between the ages of sixteen and twenty-four. During these five voyages, Jamsetji rose from being his cousin Tabak's accountant at sixteen, to being his uncle Framji's manager at eighteen and then to trading in his own right by nineteen.

Starting with his own very meagre savings, he made a fortune, mainly trading Indian cotton for Chinese tea and silk. He survived enemy gunfire, starvation and hijacking by enemy ships, and often came close to losing his life, but ended up becoming immensely rich, well known and highly respected, all by the tender age of twenty-four.

In February 1850, Jamsetji went to his native Navsari, which he had left half a century ago as a destitute and grief-stricken orphan boy. In the intervening fifty years, Jamsetji had gone from being a nonentity to becoming a national celebrity. He had travelled a long and winding road, in some places rough and thorny, and in some places smooth and spread with roses, but he was always moving upwards. On this visit to Navsari, he went to his old home and wanted to meet with a kind-hearted woman who had given him a little food for his journey when he was leaving home. He made some enquiries, and the old woman was found and he rewarded her with a large sum of money, clothes, gold coins and gold bracelets. Her kindly deed bore golden fruit fifty years later.

After earning a substantial amount of wealth, Jamsetji turned his attention to giving back to his city and community in two ways. First, he took on voluntary public works and duties, working with other young patriots, for their rights to jury duty and to be made justices of peace. Jamsetji was the first Indian to be accorded these rights. He was voted the first honorary president of the politically important Bombay Association, where Dadabhai Naoroji was making his mark. He espoused the idea of wealth earned becoming wealth shared for the common good. He built many wells, the Poona Bund and Waterworks and several dozen schools via the Sir J.J. Benevolent Institution. He also built agiaries and atash adarans, the Mahim Causeway and finally, the two magnificent crowning glories of his philanthropy, the Sir J.J. Hospital and the Sir J.J. School of Art, to which people still come to from all over India.

Sir Jamsetji Jejeebhoy was the standard bearer of far-reaching charities. He was a visionary in many respects and emphasized the importance of education. This revered leader won the love and respect of all communities by his stainless private and public life, and his business integrity raised the character of the Bombay merchant in the most distant markets of the world.

Music with a Social Responsibility

Address to the Nada Vidya Bharati Award function of the Visakha Music and Dance Academy, Visakhapatnam

14 August 2010

Our country has many talented artists and today I am happy to be in the midst of those who have rendered sustained, meritorious service and thus given happiness to the hearts of our people and to the nation. I am fully convinced that art, music, dance and drama connect the multiple levels of people in society and can elevate the minds of the people.

I once had a discussion with Pandit Jasraj and he gave me some very happy news. He said that he gave a special performance on 26 January 2007 to the inmates of the Alipore Correctional Home at Kolkata on the invitation of Shri Sharma, Inspector General of Police. Pandit Jasraj performed

Hindustani classical music for two hours, beginning with Raga Madhuvanti. The highlight of the event was the singing of bhajans like 'Om Namo Bhagavate Vasudevaya' and 'Allah Om'. I came to know that the music cheered up the inmates and gave them peace and hope.

Similarly, nadaswaram *vidwans* Sheikh Mahboob Subhani and Srimati Subhani once gave a beautiful nadaswaram recital at Rashtrapati Bhavan. At my request, both the artists gave an exclusive performance to the mentally challenged at an institute in South India. This made many of the people living there very happy. This type of social mission should be encouraged and performing artists in all parts of the country should participate in them to remove the pain of the people.

At my request, Villu Pattu Subbu Arumugam gave a performance to the inmates of the Central Prison in Chennai. Villu Pattu is a popular folk music of Tamil Nadu that deals with various social messages and also addresses mythological themes. Arumugam performed, to the inmates' delight.

Can I request all great musicians and dancers to take upon themselves a mission: the mission of using their performing art to achieve the unity of minds? I am fully convinced that if this happens, the occurrence of disturbing acts of conflict and terrorism can be reduced. Perhaps one day all of you will become successful in forming a peace team of performing artists who will offer an alternative solution to the military and judicial approach normally applied to the problems of terrorism, etc.

The Beacon of Monkhood

Address at and interaction with the UCF Open Forum, Florida, USA

2 October 2012

I once met a great sage who had performed *tapasya* for nearly eight decades. Through this intense *tapasya*, he freed himself from passion, anger, love and hate. The presence of such great souls in the country helps to spread peace and promote spiritual prosperity. He was a beacon of light that attracted people towards him to become enlightened souls. India was fortunate to have Acharya Mahaprajnaji to touch millions of souls. Even though he is no longer physically with us, he is spiritually guiding millions of followers.

I found in him three characteristics of his *tapasya*: walk, acquire and give. He walked with undeterred dedication and concentration, acquired knowledge from everyone he met, as well as from nature, and radiated hope to society through his writings, actions and practice. He was a towering inferno of knowledge that purified every soul that came into contact with him. I myself experienced this when I met Acharya Mahaprajnaji at the Adhyatma Sadhna Kendra in Mehrauli in 1999.

When I met him at midnight, he prayed three times with his distinguished Jain munis for the welfare of the nation and the people. After the prayers, I still remember, he gave me a divine message that still reverberates in my mind. He said, 'Kalam, God bless you for what you have done with your team. The Almighty has a bigger mission for you and that is why you are here with me today. I know our country is a nuclear nation now. Your mission is greater than what you and your team have done, and it is greater than what any human being has ever done. Nuclear weapons are proliferating in tens of thousands in the world. I command, with all the divine blessings, you and only you to find a solution to make the same nuclear weapons ineffective, insignificant and politically inconsequential.' When Acharyaji finished his great advice, there was silence; it seemed to me as though the heavens had concurred with the sagely message.

This command shook me and I felt this way for the first time in the sixty-eight years I had been alive. It became a challenge that kept working on me, and a motto for my life.

The Help of a Friend

Special address at the Madras Institute of Technology Alumni Association, Chennai

11 August 2012

I would like to share three incidents from the life of Chinnaswamy Rajam, the founder of the Madras Institute of Technology (MIT). The first incident took place when Rajam was a young man, twenty-seven years old. He was looking for a livelihood after experimenting with several other professions earlier. Since Madras did not offer him an opportunity, he moved back to Kumbakonam and applied to Mysore Tanneries for the position of an agent selling their products. Mysore Tanneries wanted an advance of Rs 250 which was very difficult for the young man to raise. Rajam was helped by a friend who gave him the money without any conditions attached and without even a promissory note. The availability of the money really transformed Rajam's life. He discovered his core competence: selling—or what you can also call marketing nowadays. This core competence made Rajam a successful entrepreneur and also gave him the benefits of his hard work. He became an important business leader.

As life has its way, he had a setback when his wife passed away when he was sixty-two years old. It was a major transition for him and all he wanted was to detach himself from worldly life. He sold both his bungalows and gave a donation of Rs 5 lakh to start the Madras Institute of Technology. Why did he do so? Rajam had found when he was starting electric supplies companies, he had to install a lot of electric equipment in many different places. After installation and use, some equipment inevitably had to be repaired. Every time this happened, Rajam found that he had to invite foreign technologists and technicians to set the equipment right.

Rajam wondered why Indian engineers could not design and build equipment and plants and carry out maintenance for the machines. He thought that the design, development, maintenance and operation of engineering systems should be integrated in technological fields of study. This was the inspiration that led to the founding of MIT. This process has become an integrated part of the education at MIT and MIT has generated over 20,000 engineers and technologists who are engaged in various important missions in India and abroad.

I See You

Address to and interaction with the doctors, optometrists, paramedics and staff of Sankara Nethralaya, Chennai

7 February 2013

I have attended many functions organized by eye hospitals in India and abroad and once, on the invitation of my friend Dr Umang Mathur of Dr Shroff's Charity Eye Hospital in Delhi, I participated in a function where the hospital honoured donor families. I saw hundreds of families responsible for arranging the donation of their kin's eyes to people needing corneal transplants. When I saw such good-hearted families, I felt that these are the kind of people who nurture society. That nutrient—the act of giving—offers light to a person in need, resulting in a new, bright life.

In this meeting of donors, there was mention of a unique case. A carpenter lost his life due to an electric shock. His parents readily agreed to donate his eyes, which were used for two youths on the waiting list. These two boys got corneas at Dr Shroff's Charity Eye Hospital and were able to see again. The whole experience is a beautiful phenomenon for the two boys. And, the donor's family's grief was also eased by giving light to two sightless patients.

When I heard this real-life experience, I asked the hospital authorities why they hadn't brought the two recipients to this gathering of honouring donors' families so that they could share their great happiness. I also suggested that they make a short film depicting the action, response and the happiness of the donors' families, the beneficiaries and their families. The authorities of Dr Shroff's Charity Eye Hospital, however, told me that they were forbidden by law from letting the donor family know to whom the cornea had been donated, or letting the recipient and the recipient's family know whose cornea he or she had received.

It would be useful to evolve a donor-recipient-and-hospital-friendly law that would motivate more families to come forward and donate in large numbers and bring happiness to society. This is vital to bridge the need-availability gap for corneal transplants.

Healing the Wounded

Address to and interaction with the students of Peking University, Beijing, China

3 November 2012

Through my life, I have been part of pre-Independence India, the jubilation of Independence and the post-Independence era. Let me tell you a story that took place on the eve of Indian independence. At the stroke of the midnight hour of 14 August 1947, the first Prime Minister of India, Pandit Jawaharlal Nehru, declared our independence from foreign rule to 300 million Indians. There was rejoicing all over the country.

Then suddenly, someone asked where Mahatma Gandhi, the father of the nation, was at that time. To the surprise of the entire audience, Mahatma Gandhi was in Calcutta wiping the tears of those who were affected by social disharmony.

The greatness of the Mahatma was his simplicity and his urge to serve the needy. On the momentous occasion of the independence celebrations, he was not in the midst of the pomp and show, but healing the wounded.

On another occasion, Mahatma Gandhi's diary records his advice to a group of students who came to meet him in Calcutta, 'Students ought to think, and think well. They should do no wrong . . . Students should do everything to build up a new state of India which will be everybody's pride and joy.' These actions of the champion of non-violence made me feel proud of being led by an inspirational leader.

Real Education

Address to and interaction with students at the Sri Venkateshwara Temple, Minneapolis, USA

23 May 2013

When I see you all in such a beautiful environment, I remember my schooldays in British India at the Rameswaram Panchayat Primary School from 1936 to 1944. This school was near the seashore, half-brick and half-thatch and it was the only school on Rameswaram island in those days. We were 400 boys and girls. Here is my experience, what I felt about my school, with its unimpressive building and scant amenities. I used to see an interesting scene in the school. The teachers, particularly the history, geography and science teachers, were loved by the students. Why? It's because the teachers loved their jobs and ensured the growth of each of the fifty-five students in my class. My history and geography teacher, Kaliswara Iyer, used to say, 'My students, my teaching mission is to ensure that you children love history and geography, so that you score good marks, apart from learning with pleasure.' My science teacher, Sivasubramania Iyer, was a big attraction for all the students in the class. When he entered the class in the morning, we saw the light of knowledge radiating from him.

We saw the light of purity shining in our teachers. We were fifty-five students in the eighth standard. If even one student was absent for a day, our teachers would go to the parents and enquire about the student's welfare and the reason for his or her absence. If a student got high marks, the teacher would be the first person to go to their home and share the information with their parents. My school was a happy school and all fifty-five of my classmates completed the eighth standard. I don't remember even a single dropout.

The message I would like to give this audience is that it is not a great building, great facilities or great advertisements that give you quality education, but a loving education from great teachers does. Education cannot be a business or system. Education at all levels has to be delivered in an integrated way by great teachers through a great syllabus, while promoting affinity between the parents, students and the teachers.

Failure Is a Teacher

'Dr Kalam always said success was something to be celebrated, but he also believed that failure was something that you must concentrate all your energies on resolving. He believed that failure was a teacher. This was the kind of philosophical approach he brought to problem-solving.'

G. Madhavan Nair, Former Chairman, ISRO

A Lost Scholarship

Address to and interaction with the students of Delhi Public School, Aligarh

2 November 2010

Let me tell you about Srinivasa Ramanujan, who was a genius well ahead of his time. Born and raised in Erode, Tamil Nadu, he first encountered formal mathematics at the age of ten. He demonstrated a natural ability for mathematics and was given books on advanced trigonometry by S.L. Loney. He mastered these books by age thirteen and even discovered theorems of his own. He demonstrated unusual mathematical skills at school, winning many awards. By the age of seventeen, Ramanujan was conducting his own mathematical research on Bernoulli numbers and the Euler-Mascheroni constant. He received a scholarship to study at Government College in Kumbakonam. However, he failed his non-mathematical coursework and lost his scholarship.

Ramanujan lived only for thirty-two years and did not have formal higher education or a means of living. Yet, his inexhaustible spirit and love for his subject made him contribute to the treasure houses of mathematical research, particularly in number theory. Some of his theories are still under serious study and engaging all the available efforts of the world's mathematicians to establish formal proofs.

Ramanujan was a unique Indian genius who melted the heart of the outstanding, if hardened, Cambridge mathematician Prof. G.H. Hardy. In fact, it is not an exaggeration to say that it was Prof. Hardy who discovered Ramanujan's genius for the world. Once, Prof. Hardy rated various geniuses on a scale of hundred. While most of the mathematicians got a rating of around thirty with some rare exceptions reaching to sixty, Ramanujan got a rating of hundred. There cannot be any better tribute to either Ramanujan or to Indian culture.

Ramanujan's works cover vast areas including prime numbers, hyper-geometric series, modular functions, elliptic functions, mock theta functions, even magic squares, apart from serious works on the geometry of ellipses, squaring the circle, etc. One of the tributes to Ramanujan states that 'every integer is a personal friend of Ramanujan's. He was elected a Fellow of the Royal Society in 1918.

Ramanujan used to say, 'An equation means nothing to me unless it expresses a thought of God.' For him, the understanding of numbers was a process of spiritual revelation and connection. In his investigations into pure mathematics, he drew extraordinary conclusions that mystified his colleagues, but were eventually proven to be right. He opened a universe of theory that till today is reaping applications. The landscape of the infinite was to Ramanujan a reality of both mathematics and spirit and his love for numbers led him to number theory. Despite chronic health problems, he was consumed by mathematics throughout his short life without failure ever deterring him.

The Crash

Public lecture and interaction at the DMC Auditorium, Darbhanga

23 December 2012

When you set out on difficult missions, they often bring difficult challenges that may sometimes produce temporary setbacks. The test of humanity is accepting failure and continuing to try until you achieve success. Managing failure is the ability that is the essence of leadership. Let me now share an experience in this regard from my professional life.

When I think of Prof. Satish Dhawan, many instances of his leadership come to mind. I was project director for the first experimental launch of SLV-3. On 10 August 1979, the vehicle took off beautifully at T-0 and the first stage went as predicted. The second stage was initiated but, within a few seconds, we witnessed the vehicle tumbling and we lost the flight in the Bay of Bengal. It was 8 a.m. The whole team—despite having worked all through the previous day and night, in addition to many preceding days of hard work—was busy collecting data and trying to establish the reason for the failure. Meanwhile, I was called by Prof. Dhawan to attend a press conference. Before the press conference, Prof. Dhawan told me that he was going to handle the situation, but that I should be present along with many of the senior scientists and technologists.

The room was full of people from the media and an atmosphere of gloom was prevalent. Many questions were asked, some very powerful and thoughtful and, of course, there was criticism. Prof. Dhawan announced, 'Friends, today we had the experimental launch of SLV-3 to put the Rohini satellite in orbit. It was a partial success. It is our first mission with multiple technologies in a launch vehicle. We have proved many technologies in this launch but we still have to prove some more. We have stumbled but not fallen flat. Above all, I realize my team members have to be given all the technological support for the next mission to succeed.' Subsequently, a failure analysis board established the cause and we proceeded with the preparations for the second launch.

The second SLV-3 mission took place on 18 July 1980. It was six-thirty in the morning. The whole nation's attention was on the Sriharikota High Altitude Range (SHAR) launch complex, which has now been named after Prof. Dhawan as a tribute. The mission teams were busy during the countdown and carefully watching the flight sequence. At T-0, the vehicle took off and we witnessed a textbook trajectory. After nearly 600 seconds of the flight, I realized that every stage had given the required velocity including the fourth stage. I made an announcement, 'Mission director calling all stations. The SLV-3 has given the required velocity, and right altitude to put the satellite Rohini in orbit. Our down range stations and global stations will get the orbit of the satellite within an hour.' There was thunderous applause from the station and the visitors' gallery.

The most important thing happened after that. There was another press conference. But this time, Prof. Dhawan did not handle the press; he asked me, along with the other team members, to talk to them.

There are two messages I would like to convey here. The first is one of resilience and the courage to return from a setback. And the second is of the role of a leader in managing failure. When there is success, the leader should give credit to the team. When failure comes, the leader should absorb the failure and protect the team. I had not come across this beautiful education of failure management in any of the textbooks written by any of the institutes at that time.

Believe in Yourself

Address to the participants at the valedictory session of the seminar titled 'Global Business Bridge: Linking Kentucky and India', Kentucky, USA

9 April 2010

At a meeting, I had asked some students to highlight the most inspiring person they had come across in their lives. One of the students, Stephanie, gave a beautiful answer to this question. She said that the most inspiring person she'd met was her grandmother, Esther. She told me that her grandmother had been threatened by her boss and told not to vote for a particular presidential candidate or he would fire her. But Esther decided to boldly stand up for her beliefs and principles and told her boss in front of everyone that she would freely vote for the candidate of her choice and was not intimidated by his threat.

Indeed, as history would have it, Esther voted as per her choice, that particular presidential candidate won the elections, and of course, Esther was never fired. This is a unique example of the courage of one woman to fight for her democratic rights even if it meant defying her boss. It also shows us how great examples of leadership and courage exist within our families and friend circles and how, sometimes, we may not notice them.

Do Your Best and Leave the Rest

Special address at the Madras Institute of Technology (MIT) Alumni Association, Chennai

11 August 2012

I would like to talk about an MIT alumnus, Vidyadhar, the director of the Bangalore-based Lotus Energy Systems in a different context in the corporate world. The point that I would like to make is about the high standard of ethics in financial negotiations and, as a result, in life.

Lotus Energy Systems was shortlisted as a vendor to provide soundproofing equipment for one of India's most prominent home-grown IT giants. Lotus seemed to be technically best suited for the job. The price was the only criterion that was against them. Because of high technical requirements, Vidyadhar could not offer a lower price. Perhaps he felt that it was in the customer's interest to uphold product quality since the price difference was relatively small. Above all, he defended only his company's product performance with quality as his focus—he did not belittle his competitor's products.

The buyer became reflective and then asked curiously, 'What is your philosophy while negotiating?' Vidyadhar didn't quite know what to make of it or what to say. He said the first thing that came to his mind: 'Do your best and leave the rest; if it has to happen, it will. That is our philosophy.' When the buyer asked, 'And if it means that you lose the order?' Vidyadhar replied spontaneously, '*Dharmo rakshathi rakshitha* (righteousness protects the righteous).' This statement was a reflection of his company's ethical standards.

Despite his high ethical standards, his company lost the contract even though the company needed it to survive. Then, a year or so later, something very interesting happened. Out of the blue he got a call from the same customer. They had a plan for a TV broadcast studio and needed acoustics for the project, which was something they had not done before. 'But can you do it?' the buyer asked, eager to deal with Vidyadhar's company. Vidyadhar immediately said, 'Yes'.

From that day on, his company has done a great deal of work for the facilities infrastructure of this company across India without ever having to sit across the negotiation table again. The customer, after his earlier experience of buying sound-proofing equipment, realized that he should have accepted Vidyadhar's offer because the latter had upheld the truth that their product was of a higher quality. That event changed the customer's outlook and the fortunes of both companies turned upwards, for they were truthful and honest in their dealings with each other.

Under Pressure

Address to and interaction with the students of Peking University, Beijing, China

3 November 2012

Looking at the students of Peking University, my mind goes back nearly sixty years, to 1954–57, while I was studying at the Madras Institute of Technology (MIT), Chennai. There, I had a unique professor. His name was Prof. Srinivasan. I am sure all of you have unique professors too. When we were in the final year of study, this professor called the nine of us from the aeronautics engineering faculty and assigned us a six-month project. I was designated as the project leader. My team included students from multiple areas of aeronautical engineering. Our mission: to design a low-level attack aircraft of Mach 0.8 capability within six months. Each one of us was taught specialized subjects as a part of our course. Through this project, we were given an opportunity to work on system design, system integration and system management of an end-product.

As project leader, I was responsible for system design, system integration and system management. In addition, I was also responsible for the aerodynamics and structural design of the project. The other eight engineers in my team took up the design of propulsion, structure and material, control and guidance, the avionics and the instrumentation of the aircraft. My design teacher Prof. Srinivasan, the then director of MIT, was our guide and was teaching us aircraft design.

Prof. Srinivasan reviewed the project in the fifth month and declared our work unsatisfactory and disappointing. He didn't heed my complaints of difficulties in bringing together a project designed by multiple designers. I asked for two more months to complete the task, since I had to get the inputs from eight of my colleagues, without which I could not complete the system design.

Prof. Srinivasan said, 'Look, young man, I will give you only one month. Within this time, you should complete the project and lead the team and show an integrated design, and I will review the project again. If the project is not completed in time and to the mission requirement, your scholarship will be terminated.' This was a jolt because my scholarship was my lifeline, without which I could not continue my studies. There was no other way out but to finish the task.

My team and I worked together round the clock. We didn't sleep for many nights, working on the drawing board, skipping our dinner. We were in the last week of the schedule, with the design almost assembled, and the drawings and documentation were being prepared. Prof. Srinivasan again visited us on a Sunday after his tennis game and spent two hours in our laboratory. He was very happy; he particularly appreciated the procedure we had followed and said that the integrated design had taken good shape. He commented, 'I knew I was putting you under stress and asking you to meet a difficult deadline. You have done a great job with your system design'.

Through this review mechanism, Prof. Srinivasan really underscored the necessity of understanding the value of the time spent by each team member. He also made us understand that engineering education has to lead system design, system integration and system management. I personally realized that if something is at stake, the human mind gets ignited and the individual's working capacity gets enhanced manifold.

A Star is Born

Address at the inauguration of the 'Space Festival' organized by Bharathiyar University in collaboration with NASA, Coimbatore

9 July 2012

I would like to talk to you about the work of a scientist that enabled us to calculate how long a star can survive. Subrahmanyan Chandrasekhar, in his younger days, mastered mathematics and German. His uncle C. Ramasamy recalls, 'Chandrasekhar's performance at school, especially in mathematics, was at least three years ahead of the rest of the class. His classmates were aware of his potential and recognized that there was a genius among them.'

Chandrasekhar was a voracious reader and had read everything from Shakespeare to Thomas Hardy. His reading speed was up to a 100 pages in an hour. This speed helped him to keep up with the current scientific journals while he was in college and understand the research that was going on in the laboratories across the world. While he was studying at Presidency College, Arnold Sommerfield gave a lecture on the exciting new developments in physics. Chandrasekhar was the only individual in that audience who followed every word that the great master uttered. After the lecture, Chandrasekhar had a very useful discussion with Sommerfield.

Later, after his degree, Chandrasekhar went to Trinity College at Cambridge University. During his time at Trinity, he presented two papers to the Royal Astronomical Society. One of these presentations dealt with the theory of white dwarf stars and how the quantum mechanical properties of the electron dictate the behaviour of these stars at the end of their life cycle. Chandrasekhar's colleague Sir Arthur Eddington followed this paper with a presentation that was very critical of Chandrasekhar's results. This attack was a severe blow to Chandrasekhar and left a lifelong impression on him. As a result of the disagreement, Chandrasekhar accepted a position as a research associate at the University of Chicago offered to him by the famous American astronomer Otto Struve. Chandrasekhar stayed at the University of Chicago throughout his career.

Chandrasekhar's most famous success was the astrophysical Chandrasekhar limit. He calculated this limit while travelling by ship from India to England. The limit describes the maximum mass (~1.44 solar masses) of a white dwarf star, or the minimum mass which has to be surpassed for a star to collapse into a neutron star or black hole.

In 1947, two of Chandrasekhar's students were the doctoral candidates Tsung-Dao Lee and Chen Ning Yang from

China. Even though he maintained his office at the Yerkes Observatory in Lake Geneva, Wisconsin, Chandrasekhar would regularly drive 100 miles to Chicago to teach Lee and Yang. In 1957, these two students won the Nobel Prize in physics for their work in particle physics research. This shows Chandrasekhar's dedication and commitment to his students.

Inventions and discoveries have emanated from creative minds that have been constantly working and imagining outcomes. With imagination and ceaseless effort, all the forces of the universe must work for that inspired mind, thereby leading to inventions and discoveries. I am sure all of you will take this message and apply it in your respective fields, leading you to make inventions and discoveries needed for societal upliftment regardless of failure.

A Letter to You

Excerpt from a letter, 10 Rajaji Marg, New Delhi

18 March 2010

I have one piece of advice for students based on my own experience of writing various examinations. I wrote five important exams in my educational period—ESLC (eighth standard), SSLC (tenth standard), Intermediate (twelfth standard), BSc and DMIT (aeronautical engineering). Most of the time, the outcome was not as per my expectations. I had to even lose one year due to a paper leakage. I am saying this to bring to your mind the idea that exams and exam results are not the ultimate goal in life. If you don't perform properly the first time, you can always rewrite the examination and succeed.

Hence, I suggest to you: success always brings happiness but sometimes, we have to be prepared to go through some setbacks in examinations, which could be for a variety of reasons. I would like you to remember my teacher's advice: 'In life, we have to be prepared to go through certain unexpected problems. The problem should not become our captain. Students like you should become the captain of the problem, defeat the problem and succeed.'

The courage to succeed and the courage to face unexpected problems are the unique qualities of the youth. You will definitely succeed; go on trying. Do not get disheartened by temporary setbacks.

A Mother's Dream

Address to the students of Delhi Public School, Varanasi

14 March 2012

Let me tell you the story of Sulochana from Karnataka, who wrote to me about her mother. She said that her mother was born in a very poor family and hence was unable to achieve her dream of getting a degree—she only went to primary school. This made her resolve to educate her children so that they would get high-level degrees and work at great companies. She struggled very hard to convince Sulochana's father to put Sulochana and her sister in a good school. Her mother fasted for two to three days in order to make her father accept that the children should be put in the best school regardless of the expense.

Finally she succeeded, and in gratitude she promised that she would never ask anything else of him. She was satisfied that her children were going to get a good education, which she hadn't been able to herself. Sulochana writes, 'Now, she is very happy that I, her eldest daughter, am going to complete my engineering degree with a job in a multinational company through campus recruitment. When my mother heard that I had secured a job, she was very happy that I had fulfilled her dream. I saw her smiling at me with tears in her eyes, saying, "Congrats, my dear daughter"'. A mother's love can indeed make children excel.

Life Is Beautiful

'No President was ever loved so much. Nehru has earned the love and affection of children and after that we found Kalam. Sometimes when he was with children, it appeared to me that he is Nehru in another form. He was always inspiring new ideas, new thoughts.'

Pranab Mukherjee, President of India

Make your Mother Smile Mission

Address at the inauguration of the golden jubilee celebrations of Volontariat, Puducherry

8 June 2012

Over the past few months, the What Can I Give Mission has been taking the Make Your Mother Smile movement across the nation to a large number of young children, assigning them the unique task of ensuring that their actions make their mothers smile every day. I have given millions of children the following oath:

Make your mother smile always
If your mother smiles, the home smiles
If homes smile, society smiles
If societies smile, the nation smiles

I have come across some touching examples and stories in these missions. Allow me to share some of them with you. Dhiraj, a tenth standard student from Delhi, wrote saying that for him, a mother's love can be defined in a mathematical equation. He said,

$$\text{Mother's love} = \tan \theta, \text{ where } \theta = 90 \text{ degrees.}$$

Hence, according to this equation, his mother's love = infinity. What a beautiful way to express the love of a mother! Similarly, Riya Arora, a student of the eighth standard, defines a mother as:

M = Motivation comes with her blessings
O = An optimistic person
T = Turns tots to teens
H = Honest and best at her work
E = Enthusiasm touches her feet
R = Right she'll always be!

I thought that was a really wonderful way to define the love of a mother.

Through the What Can I Give Mission, over one million children are now engaged in the mission of making their mothers smile across the nation, spreading the idea 'When a mother smiles, society smiles'.

A Small Miracle

Address at the graduation day of Adichunchanagiri Institute of Medical Sciences, Mandya

22 March 2013

Nihar's parents suspected he had a learning disability when he was four years old, based on certain symptoms in his communication and walking and his aggressive behaviour. The parents admitted Nihar to a mainstream school, where the teachers were unable to teach the child until he was twelve. This was not of much help, so Nihar was brought to a special school. He was taken to the ITU (Intensive Therapy Unit) for the first three years, which was a great challenge. In the classroom he had zero sitting tolerance. This condition improved after his first auditory retraining. The teachers of the school worked with Nihar using the programme 'Facing learning disability through communication with the environment'. The programme had four phases.

By making the best of his environment, Nihar's innate abilities for music and art came to the fore during the third year and he showed signs of settling down and doing the work given to him in the pre-vocational classroom. He started using eye contact and could focus on what was being said to him. Due to his strong inclination towards art, he was promoted to the art department for his vocational training along with alternative therapies like yoga, laughter therapy, brain gym, etc. This phase of the programme is based on the integration of the left and the right brain, thereby developing the whole personality of the student and enabling him to overcome his disabilities to an extent.

The third phase of the programme was 'Linking and initiating a network of communication through synergy', wherein he was respected and treated as a member of society with the potential to reach greater goals. This mentoring strategy created a synergy between the mentor and the mentee, between peers and between the student and society. Here, Nihar learnt to become part of the group in the visual arts and crafts department, interacting with his peers and accompanying them on outdoor educational excursions. Nihar's behaviour changed over a period of one year.

In the last phase, the school normalized the parents' behaviour and tried to remove psychological blocks towards disability, thereby enabling the parents to become totally accountable for and participate fully in Nihar's day-to-day life. Nihar's mother had to be counselled to help her overcome her anxiety and apprehensions, which had prevented Nihar from becoming independent. She cooperated with the school programme and really worked hard with her son. Today, she is proud of Nihar and his achievements.

Nihar completed his training with that school for fourteen years before joining the Shraddha Charitable Trust and has successfully completed two years of his internship. He is an earning member of society with a salary of Rs 5000. Today, Nihar is an independent individual enjoying all the activities and competitions that he can participate in.

The message we get from Nihar's experience is that parents should admit children with learning disabilities in an appropriate school without waiting for too long. There is a need to train a large number of teachers who can handle special children and then, to place these teachers in regular schools. This will at least enable the early recognition of special needs, which will lead to admitting the child into the right environment for treatment and training.

The Real Truth

Address to the inauguration of the Interfaith Meet organized by the Ramakrishna Mission, New Delhi

10 September 2011

In 2003, I visited Arunachal Pradesh and spent nearly a whole day at a Buddhist monastery at Tawang at an altitude of 3500 metres. I saw a unique situation in all the villages nearby, where the young and the experienced were all radiating happiness in spite of the severe winter. At the 400-year-old Tawang monastery, I also saw monks of all ages in a state of serenity. I asked myself what the unique feature of Tawang and the surrounding villages was that made the people and the monks be at peace with themselves. When the time came, I asked the chief monk how everyone in the Tawang village and the monastery was so full of peace and happiness. There was a pause, and the chief monk smiled. He said, 'You are the

President of India. You must know all about us and the whole nation.' Again I said, 'It is very important to me and I would like you to please give me your thoughtful analysis.'

There was a beautiful smiling golden image of Lord Buddha radiating peace. The chief monk assembled near it with almost all of his hundred monks, young and experienced alike. We sat amidst them. The chief monk gave a short discourse, which I would like to share with you. He said, 'In the present world, we have a problem of distrust and unhappiness transforming into violence. This monastery spreads the idea that when you remove 'I' and 'me' from your mind, you will eliminate ego; if you get rid of ego, hatred towards fellow human beings will vanish; if hatred goes out of our mind, the violence in thought and action will disappear; if violence in our mind is taken away, peace springs in human minds. Then peace and peace and peace alone will blossom in society.'

I realized the meaning of this beautiful equation for a peaceful life but saw that removing the ethos of 'I' and 'me' would be a difficult task for the individual. We need to inculcate this idea into children from a very young age. In my search for a peaceful and prosperous society, I got a partial answer. My search for the real truth continues.

A Friend in all Seasons

Address at the Poetry Society of India, New Delhi

8 July 2011

When I meet the poet community, I'm inspired to share with you the beautiful story of a 100-year-old tree in my garden at 10, Rajaji Marg. The tree is called Arjuna, while botanically its name is *Terminalia arjuna*. The tree is my biodiversity friend. I walk for about one and a half hours every morning and night in my garden. My tree friend reveals something new to me every day. You might ask how one single 100-year-old tree can become a living symbol for biodiversity. The tree and my parents are almost the same age. My father lived 103 years and my mother more than ninety. To my sorrow, my tall friend Arjuna, with hundreds of branches, loses all his leaves and becomes barren every April. Then, to my joy, within a month he blossoms with more vigour and fresh green leaves and colourful flowers, making him look even mightier.

There are hundreds of branches in the tree. There is one branch which particularly difficult to locate, as it is in the dense interior region of the tree. On that branch, I saw a unique sight: thousands and thousands of working honeybees have built a huge hive. Many parts of Arjuna have become the habitat for mynahs, sparrows, black crows and cuckoos, with the topmost branches occupied by beautiful parakeets. Occasionally, a hornbill visits, and then all the other birds join together to drive away this species. Every day I observe how all the birds join together against their common enemy, the kite, in order to protect their young ones.

My tree gives beautiful shade to all living beings in all seasons. Many times, I have seen peacocks dancing in numbers around the tree. Then the peahen selects a bush around the tree to lay seven to ten eggs, which she protects for forty-five days, sitting softly on the eggs, keeping them warm.

Don't you think I have a great tree? It is my biodiversity friend and also a friend of the young. I wrote a poem dedicated to Arjuna, my home tree. I asked my tree: What is your mission? You may like to hear the great answer my home tree gave me.

A.P.J. Abdul Kalam

The Great Tree in My Home

Oh, my home tree,
You are great among trees,
How many, many generations were enriched
Through decades of your help, so kind,
Many now live under your sagely care,
Your song of life, I love to hear.

Oh, my friend Kalam,
I crossed the age of hundred like your father and mother.
Every morning, you walk an hour
I also see you on full moon nights,
Walking in a thinking mood.
I know, my friend, the thoughts in your mind,
'What can I give you?'
When in April, you look at me,
Again and again with deep concern,
Seeing me shedding leaves in thousands and thousands,
You ask me, my friend,
What is my burden?
Leaves I shed to give birth to new leaves,
Flowers bloom attracting butterflies and bees.
So, Kalam, it is not a burden for me,
It is a beautiful phase of my life.
Now, Kalam, take a tour with me,
See closely inside, in my dense branches,
A large beehive full of honey,

My India: Ideas for the Future

Built by thousands of worker bees,
Honey collected by their ceaseless work.
A honey hive so heavy, with sweet honey drops,
Guarded well by thousands of bees.
For whom is this honey collected and guarded?
It is for you many rich and poor,
Our mission is to give to every life.
Oh, Kalam, did you see so many nests,
Built by various birds in various parts of my branches?
Most of the top branches of my tree attract
Hundreds of parrots as their home.
You have rightly called me the parrots' tree.
Nowadays, you also call me honey tree,
When I hear you talking to your grandson about me,
I smile and smile.
I give many homes to birds in my branches and trunk holes.
I have heard songs of birds, and seen love, birth and growth.
The birds are flying and flying around me sharing happiness.
Nowadays, Kalam, daily during your walk,
You come close to me to see my roots,
All around the dense flower garden with a velvet grass bed
To a peahen,
The peahen giving warmth to the eggs,
All the time giving safe breeding with motherly love.
It was a beautiful sight in your home.
The peahen with her seven kids,
Majestically walking now all around me,
And guarding the children day and night.

A.P.J. Abdul Kalam

Now, you question, Kalam, what is my mission?
The mission of the hundred years of my life?
My mission, I enjoy giving what all I have,
I share flowers and honey, give an abode to hundreds of birds.
I give and give. So, I remain young and happy, always.

The Magic of Science

Address at the inauguration of Truth Labs, an independent forensic laboratory, Chennai

10 July 2010

The emergence of new technologies from research laboratories and their spread through society is a beautiful thing. The advances in biological sciences and the growth in biotechnology have had a significant impact on various areas of society including industry, government policies and the judiciary. Forensic science is one of the tools that helps to establish efficiency and accuracy in the judicial system, and the judiciary forms the basis of our social fabric and is the basic building block of our nation.

Recently, I read an article that highlighted the innovation and expansion of the spectrum of inputs that can be used for forensic science. The article discussed an experiment being conducted by Prof. Noah Fierer and his research team at the University of Colorado, which analyzed the scope of hand bacteria in forensic identification. The team took swabs from keyboards of computers and were able to match the bacteria they found to the owners of the computers. They found, as reported in the BBC, 'every person leaves behind a unique trail of bugs as they go about their daily lives'. And this trail, these scientists say, could be the basis of a new forensic tool.

Even on a clean hand, there would be about 150 species of bacteria. The research team matched the samples with random people and observed accuracy up to 90 per cent. The most promising aspect is that hand bacteria can survive for two weeks at room temperature and can be useful even when the fingerprints are smudged or insufficient DNA is available. This highlights the fact that forensic scientists have to be innovative in their approach and must constantly evolve new and more robust methods of forensic analysis that can use a wider variety of inputs. As criminals are evolving new ways to evade justice, forensics will have to constantly transform and expand its horizons.

A Beautiful Mind

Address to the differently abled children of the Lead India 2020 programme and the Government of Tamil Nadu, Coimbatore

14 December 2012

In 1970, a woman gave birth to a baby girl, Tamanna, in a well-known hospital. At that time, the hospital had no facilities for a Caesarean operation and the attending doctor insisted on a natural birth. Her labour pains started at 10 p.m. and continued up to 2 a.m. The doctor then used forceps during the delivery and that damaged the child's brain. Additionally, the prolonged labour pains caused severe hypoxic conditions for the child. As a result, Tamanna was unable to hold her head up and suckle. Her hands and legs were crossed and opened outwards.

After thirteen days, Tamanna was taken to the Post Graduate Institute of Medical Education and Research in Chandigarh. The electroencephalogram could not detect any damage and the doctor advised her mother to go to a bigger hospital. It took them two months to reach one. When they took a CT scan, they found that there was severe incurable brain damage. The doctor said, 'No improvement in her condition is possible. All that happened has happened. If anything at all can progress, she will have late or delayed milestones.'

When Tamanna was about three months old, she was taken to Dr Firoz in Mumbai and spent one year under his treatment. After this, Tamanna was taken to the US for further treatment where she underwent a lot of physiotherapy, including the use of the Swiss ball to develop the coordination of various muscles. After six long years of effort, she was finally able to stand on her own legs. Later, she also started climbing stairs with the help of the railing; she found this both easy and interesting and it helped further develop her muscles.

Tamanna's mother had begun giving her a variety of waterproof books to read. She began to read and understand them slowly. Her mother also talked to her continuously. Tamanna understood her mother, and though she was unable to respond or express her feelings in return, she was absorbing all the information. And so, the family kept on talking to her. At the age of nine, Tamanna finally started talking. Concentration and abstraction were still difficult for her. Discrimination was very difficult for her and this made her mother anxious. She was put on a rigorous course of different types of learning and work and at the age of eleven, she began to learn how to dance.

She joined Mount Carmel School and started going to school by four-wheeler. Later, she began to go by bicycle. She graduated high school from the National Open School with 68 per cent marks. She also completed a course in tourism and teacher's training from the Indira Gandhi National Open University. She continues to do some breathing exercises and pranayama. Her typical day now includes attending language development class, Western music class, Kathak class, reading the newspaper, surfing the internet, teaching at DPS and swimming. She is also trying to complete a BA programme in counselling.

Tamanna's experience clearly shows that if parents persevere and provide the right environment, medical intervention and psychological support, even the most severe cases of mentally challenged children can lead a normal life

Nurturing the Seeds

Inaugural address at the Children's Science Congress during the 101st Indian Science Congress, University of Jammu, Jammu

3 February 2014

In 2001, while I was teaching at Anna University, I was invited by Presidency College in Chennai to interact with students. When I reached the venue, I saw more than 1500 students in the hall. It was very tough to reach the dais. After I finished my lecture, 'Vision Elevates the Nation', I was asked a number of questions by the students. When I was leaving the hall, a young student suddenly came out of the crowd and thrust a crumpled piece paper into my hand. I put the paper in my pocket and read it on my way back to Anna University.

My mind was elevated by the power of the message from T. Saravanan who was pursuing an M.Phil. at Presidency College at that time. I would like to share the content of the letter with all of you. The letter went like this:

My India: Ideas for the Future

Dear Kalam sir, the power of the banyan tree is equal to the power in the seeds of the tree. In a way, the both of us, you and me, are the same, but we exhibit our talents in different forms. A few of the seeds become banyan trees but many seeds die as saplings without ever becoming a tree. Due to certain circumstances and environmental conditions, many seeds even get damaged and become part of the soil as fertilizer and help new seeds to become trees.

Saravanan then went on to ask, 'You have worked for the country and helped many scientists, engineers and knowledge workers, can you tell me how you ensured that their abilities were not wasted or their growth was not stunted prematurely like banyan seeds that never become trees? What is the percentage of success you can claim?'

I replied and told Saravanan that it was my great joy to see my team members excelling in terms of both knowledge and achievement. Regarding the percentage of success, I think that it must be at least 60 per cent. But this 60 per cent emerged from the 100 per cent who worked on the projects.

The message I would like to give is: the seeds of the banyan tree are indeed like the citizens of the nation. Democracy and governance have the power to provide growth opportunities to every citizen with the capacity to perform. Every citizen, therefore, has the capacity to contribute to the vision of the country in his or her own way and, in the process, contribute to the success of what seems like a few. And this can grow in geometric proportion and result in the success of India, which is a success that will be shared by all Indian citizens. Let us nurture every seed. We should always remember, however, that seeds which become manure must not be considered any lesser than seeds that become trees.

The Dual Role of Music

Address at The Hindu Saregama M.S. Subbulakshmi Award ceremony, Chennai

11 April 2011

Music has the power to cheer a person in spite of any handicap, be it physical or visual. But the most important aspect is how much happiness can be derived by singing for others. I have witnessed this on two occasions which I would like to share with you.

During the Sangeet Natak Akademi Awards in 2005, I was about to give the award to Srimati Gayathri Sankaran, a visually challenged lady. She whispered in my ear, 'May I sing for you?'

I said, 'Of course, you can sing for a minute.' And then she sang a beautiful Thyagaraja krithi. The second occasion was when, during a recent visit, I was meeting people from various walks of life in Coimbatore. One person entered in a wheelchair. He had no legs and no hands and yet, he was radiating happiness and cheer. 'What makes him so cheerful,' I asked myself.

I learnt that his name was Vidwan S.R. Krishnamurthy. I asked him, 'Please tell me, what can I do for you?' He surprised me by saying, 'I want to sing for you at Rashtrapati Bhavan.' Then, he told me about how he had started his music lessons with his sister and later continued his training under Meenakshiammal, a disciple of Vidwan Tiger Varadachari. He added that he was a Grade A artist at All India Radio and had won many awards. He taught music from his home and had given many concerts. I observed one significant thing as he spoke to me: he kept smiling and was extremely grateful to all those who had helped him on his way. After the discussion, he sang a beautiful krithi.

This is another example of how music has played a beautiful dual role. In this unique case, music had helped him conquer his ego and helped take away the pain of a physical handicap. In giving music to others, he derived happiness, which made him cheerful. It is a great lesson for all of us.

An Inherited World

Address to and interaction with the students of UCF, Orlando, USA

27 September 2012

Wangari Muta Maathai was born in Nyeri, Kenya, in 1940. She was the first woman in East and Central Africa to earn a doctorate and to become an associate professor and later, the chair of a department in a university (the Department of Veterinary Anatomy). Wangari Maathai was active in the National Council of Women of Kenya (NCWK) and was chairperson in 1981-87. She continued to develop the NCWK into a broad-based, grassroots organization whose main focus is the planting of trees for women's groups in order to conserve the environment and improve the quality of life.

Thus was born the Green Belt Movement, where women would be given one shilling for each exotic tree they distributed and two shillings for indigenous/fruit trees. Prof. Maathai has innovatively evolved a movement with 600 community networks across Kenya and branches in twenty countries, resulting in the planting of thirty-one million trees. She and the Green Belt Movement have received numerous awards, most notably the Nobel Peace Prize in 2004.

Prof. Maathai gives a new meaning to the important act of planting a tree by extending it to the whole of life when she says, 'The planting of trees is the planting of ideas'. She highlights the qualities of patience, persistence and commitment in planning and realizing a future, which is what we learn when we plant trees and wait for them to yield fruits for the next generation. She believes that no matter how dark the cloud, there is always a thin silver lining, and that is what we must look for. The silver lining will come, if not to us, then to the next generation or the generation after that. And maybe for that generation, the lining will no longer be thin.

India values Prof. Maathai's involvement in and contribution to furthering the relationship between India and Kenya and had the privilege of honouring her with the Jawaharlal Nehru Award for International Understanding for 2005. She concluded the Nobel Lecture on 10 December 2004 as follows, 'As I conclude, I reflect on my childhood experience when I would visit a stream next to our home to fetch water for my mother. I would drink water straight from the stream. I saw thousands of tadpoles: black, energetic and wriggling through the clear water against the background of the brown earth. This is the world I inherited from my parents.'

And all of us should preserve this inheritance.

The Most Cherished Moment

Address to the participants of the Prof. Bijayanand Patnaik Memorial Lecture, Bhubhaneswar

15 January 2012

On New Year's Day, I met my friend Dr Taraprasad Das at my home in the evening. He is well-known for having cured more than 300 patients using his research in stem cell treatment, based on the cells taken from the patient's eye. While we were reviewing our experiences in the past year, I asked my friend about what unique things had happened in the year gone by that he would always remember. For my part, I told him about one unique experience in 2010, which was seeing my friend, V. Kathiresan, who used to work for me as my driver. He had since earned a PhD degree and was now a lecturer.

I also recalled the evolution of World Vision 2030, which I had put together with my team and my students from the Gatton College of Business and Economics (University of Kentucky) and the Indian Institutes of Management at Ahmedabad and Indore. Then, Dr Das told me about his unique achievements in the past year. First, he told me that more than 1,32,000 patients had been treated in various hospitals under his direct management. He said that a doctor's most cherished moment is when a patient recovers fully with the treatment administered. He then told me a story.

A patient from Dubai, Krishna Pathak, wanted to be treated by Dr Das. The patient had gone through multiple treatments in many places, including abroad. He also had multiple eye diseases, including diabetic retinopathy and macular oedema, which had affected both his eyes. These resulted in the loss of sight and he could no longer read and write. After diagnosis, Dr Das treated Mr Pathak with several injections inside the eyes and laser treatments. His vision, after a few months of treatment, improved greatly and he could see and read. Mr Pathak, on the day he was discharged from the hospital, asked Dr Das, 'What dreams do you have? You know, Dr Das, I am a well-to-do person and can help you fulfil your dreams.' Dr Das told him, 'I would like to establish an eye institute and a research laboratory in Bhubaneswar, whose focus would be on diabetic retinopathy coupled with stem cell research.'

Mr Pathak, with all happiness, said, 'Oh, Dr Das, I will sponsor this research facility with a sum of one million US dollars. I would also like you to impart training to students and create many more Dr Dases.' My own assessment is that Dr Das, a healthcare giver, got double recognition—for diagnosis and cure coupled with compassion and service for the patient.

We Are One

Address at the launch of Hinduism: An Introduction *at the Akshardham Temple, New Delhi*

1 July 2011

When I was reading *Hinduism: An Introduction*, particularly on prayers relating to the Gayatri Mantra, I recalled an experience which I would like to share with you. One of my friends, Dhan Shyam Sharma, always chants a mantra every morning after his bath, whether he is in Delhi or any other city in India or abroad. One day, I asked Dhan Shyam what he was chanting. He told me that he recited the Gayatri Mantra every day at least 108 times after bathing.

On some special occasions, he chanted the mantra over 216 times. I asked him to chant the Gayatri Mantra in my presence and he chanted it beautifully. I asked him about the meaning of this mantra and he explained the meaning as he understood it. When I read the second part of *Hinduism: An Introduction*, I got the full meaning, that is:

> *(We meditate on) Om (which pervades) earth,*
> *Intervening space and swarga (heaven)*
> *May we contemplate on the desirable radiance of*
> *The sun god; May he guide our intellects.*

The author also says that the title Gayatri Mantra literally means 'the mantra that protects the one who chants it'. Chanting the Gayatri Mantra invokes dignity and blesses one with spiritual illumination, cosmic energy, intelligence, subtle discrimination, creative vision and healing powers.

The prayer is chanted three times a day, following the changing position of the sun in the sky. When I think about the chanting of this mantra, I am reminded of my own schedule of prayer, the namaz, which is done five times a day with the verse:

> *Bismillâhi r-rahmâni r-rahîm*
> *Al hamdu lillâhi rabbi l-'âlamîn*
> *Ar rahmâni r-rahîm*
> *Mâliki yawmi d-dîn*
> *Iyyâka na'budu wa iyyâka nasta'în*
> *Ihdinâ ṣ-ṣirâṭ al-mustaqîm*
> *Ṣirâṭ al-laḏîna an'amta 'alayhim ġayril*
> *maġḍûbi 'alayhim walaḍ ḍâllîn*

This means:

In the name of God, the most beneficent, the most merciful
All appreciation, gratefulness and thankfulness are to Allah alone, Lord of the worlds.
The most beneficent, the most merciful
The possessor of the day of judgement.
You we worship, and from you we seek help
Direct all of us to the straight path.
The way of those on whom you have bestowed your grace,
Not the way of those who have earned your anger,
Nor of those who have lost their way and are astray.

As we can see, both the prayers seek blessings and guidance so that an individual always follows the path of right conduct as prescribed in the principles of dharma.

Books Are Our Companions

Address at the 20th New Delhi World Book Fair, New Delhi

3 March 2012

Coming into contact with a good book and owning it is indeed an everlasting enrichment of life. The book becomes a permanent companion. Sometimes, books are born before us; they guide us during the journeys of our lives and continue to do so for many generations. I had bought a book titled *Light from Many Lamps* in 1953 from an old bookstore in Moore Market in Chennai. The editor of this book is Lillian Eichler Watson.

This book has been my close friend and companion for more than five decades. The book was used so much that it had to be re-bound many times. I realized the importance of the book again when a friend of mine who is in the judiciary presented me with the new edition of the same book recently. He told me the best thing he could give me was this book because of how much I loved it. And perhaps fifty years from now, the same book may take a new avatar. Hence, books are eternal and powerful.

Read More in Puffin

Reignited: Scientific Pathways to a Brighter Future
A.P.J. Kalam and Srijan Pal Singh

Will robots take over the world? When will we meet aliens? How are memories stored inside the brain?

Join A.P.J. Kalam on a fascinating quest to explore the realm of science and technology, its extraordinary achievements and its impact on our lives in the days to come. Co-written with Srijan Pal Singh, this book features exciting and cutting edge career paths in areas such as robotics, aeronautics, neurosciences, pathology, palaeontology and material sciences in other words, careers that are going to make a difference in the future. The result of extensive research, this book offers a plethora of ground-breaking ideas that will make youngsters think out of the box.

Read More in Puffin

Mission India: A Vision for India Youth
A.P.J. Kalam with Y.S Rajan

'Each and every Indian can make a difference, especially the nation's youth'

Mission India: A Vision for Indian Youth has been written with the intention of challenging the Indian youth to bring about a positive change in the country by 2020.

A.P.J. Kalam and Y.S Rajan tell readers about their goal to make India one among the five top economic powers in the world by 2020. In the beginning of this book, Kalam asks readers whether India can become a developed country. He then provides insights into the current situation in the country, and explains that this goal is a realistic one. In subsequent chapters, Kalam and Rajan examine the five industries that need to become reasonably self-sufficient in the coming years, and they tell readers what can be done to bring a positive change in each industry.

Kalam and Rajan conclude by detailing the role every individual and organization can play in transforming the nation by 2020.

18D
27/9/11